T0047238

الله
محمد
علی
فاطمة
حسن
حسین

"In the Name of God, the Beneficent, the Merciful"

The book describes patience as the key for building an ideal Islamic society. Without patience the truth and steadfast logic of the exalted school of religion wouldn't have been understood. Also it contains a detailed commentary about the philosophy of daily ritual prayer in Islam. The writer describes the Prayer of Islam like a siren for awakening us; a warning at different hours of the day and night which provides a program for human beings, requiring their commitment for its execution.

Importance of Patience and Prayer

Lectures of:
Grand Ayatollah Sayyid Ali Khamenei
Supreme Leader of I.R. Iran

Translated From the Persian By:
Sayyid Hussein Alamdar

authorHOUSE®

AuthorHouse™
1663 Liberty Drive
Bloomington, IN 47403
www.authorhouse.com
Phone: 1 (800) 839-8640

Published by AuthorHouse 03/09/2016

ISBN: 978-1-5049-7107-2 (sc)
ISBN: 978-1-5049-7108-9 (hc)
ISBN: 978-1-5049-7106-5 (e)

Library of Congress Control Number: 2015921377

Print information available on the last page.

This book is printed on acid-free paper.

"The Holy Prophet (SAW) has said: 'I am leaving two heavy trust among you—The Book of God and my Ahl al-Bayt—until you remain attached to these two, you would never be deviated. Verily these two would never be separated from each other until they see me at the Fountain of Kauther.'"

—Sahih Muslim v.7, p-122; Sinnan Darmi v.2, p-432; Masnad Ahmad v.3, p-14, 17, 26; v. 4, p-371; v. 5, p-182, 189; Musadarik Hakim, v. 3, p-109, 148, 533.

"O the People of House—the Holy Prophet's (SAW) Ahl al-Bayt (AS), God has made your love in the Holy Qu'ran as compulsory."

"This pride is sufficient—that if the salutations are not offered upon you in the daily prayers they are not acceptable by God."

—Imam Shaf'aie.

Acknowledgment

I have known Sayyid Hussein Alamdar for several years, what can I say about him? He is an element that does not need recognition. A tradition narrated to our great Holy Prophet (SAW) that said: ***"People are like metals, such gold and silver,"*** by one look you can recognize and at least guess the gold from other metals. Today, the languages that have established themselves in benefiting from Islam, are definitely Arabic and the second language I say is Persian, we have a great flow of information from Islam, it is an eternal spring, truly as a great eternal spring, but who is going to carry that knowledge to other non Arabic or Persian speakers? Usually if you see a book in Arabic, chances are you see it in Persian, you seldom see them in other languages. Since unfortunately very little of that spring is going to Europe or the West, or let us say to English speaking nations. Not only that, but because of the ignorance about Islam, the media, is fighting forcefully to destroy this spring and to distort the beautiful picture of Islam, as a matter fact, the TV and other media became so successful that today a Muslim is looked at as a guilty terrorist, even though the law said: ***"A man is innocent until proven guilty!"***

Mr. Alamdar, bravely at this era—the era of such a media (and other means of fight) is going single handedly against this huge flow. He is exerting all of his efforts, time, and using his pen to spread the traditions of his grand fathers, fourteen precious, errorless and infallibles imams (AS) to the English speaking populations. At the time that I met him, his reputation had already reached me, the translation of the book of Imam Hussein (AS) was already published and spread, since then determinedly and diligently, writing about the progeny of the Holy Prophet (SAW), books as the lives of the Imams (AS). Also translations of the books that will lift your spiritual life to the moral life and rise your spirit to the highest level, after all, the spiritual life is far more important than the physical life, although both are important, yet the body has a due date on it and will expire at a certain specific time but, but the spirit has an eternal life as Allah (SWT) said in many verses in the Holy Qur'an.

These books are:

1. Radiance of Vicegerency *(Froogh-e-Vilayat)*: Grand Ayatollah J'afar Sobhanie, 2. Fatimeh al-Zahra (SA), 3. Imam Zain al-A'abedin (AS), 4. Imam Muhammad al-Baqir (AS), 5. Imam J'afar al-Sadiq (AS): Hujjatul Islam Wal Muslimin, Sayyid Munthir Hakim, 6. Self Building, 7. Every Body Must Know: Ayatollah Ibrahim Amini, 8. Truth and Falsehood and Renaissance of Islamic Thought: Martyr Ustad Murtaza Motaheri (RA), 9. The Story of Karbala: Ayatollah Ali Nazari Munfarid, 10. Biography of Sayyid Razi: Hujjatul Islam Wal Muslimin Muhammad Ibrahim Nejad, 11. Etiquettes of the Holy Month of Ramadhan *(Suluk-e-Aarifan)*: Grand Ayatollah Javad Agha Maliki Tabrizi (RA), 12. Importance of Patience and Prayer, 13. A 250 years Old Human Being: Grand Ayatollah Sayyid Ali Khamenei, 14. A Dialogue Between a Father and Son: Ayatollah Sayyid Muhammad Taqi Hakim, 15. History of the Holy Mosque of Jamkaran.

I think these books should be read, whether, they are the lives of the Impeccable Imams (AS), the models and the perimeters of our lives to be followed, or the moral issues, Mr. Alamdar is greatly needed in this field of translation. May Allah (SWT) accept and give him the strength to continue this deed.

Dr. M. Jowad Al-Ansari

Clinical Pastoral Psychology, Detroit, MI (USA)

Dedication

"In the Name of God, the Beneficent, the Merciful."

O God! It was Thy grace and blessing upon this humble servant to translate this book: Importance of Patience and Prayer by Grand Ayatollah Sayyid Ali Khamenei from Persian into English. If this work deserves to earn Your reward please bestow upon the souls of all innocent victims of global terrorism, recent massacre of thousands of Shi'i Muslims in Nigeria, and especially exalted martyr and prominent Shi'i scholar Ayatollah Sheik Baqir Nimr al-Nimr (RA) who was assassinated on Jan 2, 2016 by the criminal House of al-Saud of KSA in spite of serious opposition shown by all international human rights organizations and UN. May Your curse and wrath be upon those who are fully supporting and backing openly and secretly the global terrorists namely: ISIL, ISIS, Daesh, al-Qaida, al-Nusra, Jaysh al-Islam, Taliban, Al-Shahab, Boka Haram, and all the worlds most despicable, murderous, inhuman, heinous, and barbaric terror groups. And may Your blessing be upon all the noble statesmen and peace makers of the world who are sincerely and courageously fighting with this intentionally and artificially created evil of global terrorism in any form. And salutations be upon all the epic martyrs of humanity who sacrificed their precious lives in fighting with these tyrants for the sake of freedom, honor, justice, peace, prosperity, coexistence, and human dignity all over the world.

Contents

Part-1: Patience

1. Translator's Foreword–Patience

One of the most brilliant, gifted and worthy sons of Islam of our age; a great scholar, thinker, philosopher, jurisprudent, writer of great intellect, defender of honor of Islam during the deposed Pahlavi regime; and best pupil and outcome of the entire life of Imam Khomeini (RA)—Martyr Ayatollah Sheikh Murtaza Motaheri (RA)—who was martyred on May 1, 1979 by the terrorist Furqan group in Tehran—has said regarding the need of publishing suitable Islamic literature as follows:

"We are responsible people, we have not produced sufficient literature in various aspects of Islam in the current languages. Had we therefore made available pure and sweet waters in abundance, people would not have contented themselves with polluted waters."[1]

Keeping the above in mind, I have tried to translate the book: Importance of Patience and Prayer in Islam by Grand Ayatollah Sayyid Ali Khamenei from Persian into English, as my insignificant contribution to produce a tiny drop of pure and sweet water. He delivered these speeches during Muharram of 1394 AH, 1973 AD at Masjid-e-Karamat, in the City of Mashad, Khorasan, I.R. Iran. The speeches contain valuable information in accordance the Holy Qur'an's verses, Holy Prophet's (SAW), and Ahl al-Bayt's (AS) most authentic traditions about the importance of patience. These books were first published in the form of two separate books namely: Discourse on Patience *(Guftari der Bareyeh Sabr)* and Profundities of Prayer *(Azh Zharfhai Namaz).* My earlier English translations of these books were published by Ansariyan Publications of Qum,

---

[1] Islamic Movements in Twentieth Century by Martyr Ayatollah Motaheri (RA).

I.R. Iran in the year 1994 and since then their several editions have been published. Now, it was considered appropriate to combine these two books into a single book under the title of: Importance of Patience and Prayer in Islam. As the writer of these books Grand Ayatollah Khamenei has stated: ***"An indifferent, unaware believer could be compared to a soldier in the battlefield, who is fighting naked without wearing armor. Such an ill-equipped soldier is most likely to be killed or disappear from the scene during the very first encounter. However an aware, conscientious, and knowledgeable Muslim with Islamic ideology could be compared to a soldier—who is fully clad in armor from head to foot and is fully equipped with all the required armaments. Obviously, for the enemy to defeat such a well equipped soldier is a relatively difficult task."*** [1]

The struggle between the total belief and blasphemy is going on fiercely on all fronts namely: Militarily, economically, and culturally. The most severe among them is the cultural onslaught being waged by those who worship the darkness or devil, don't believe in God's existence,[2] life after death, hereafter, day of resurrection, and accounting of deeds etc. This ideological and

---

1. Importance of Patience and Prayer by Grand Ayatollah Khamenei.

2. Therefore, if Islam proposes liberty, freedom, justice, human friendship, and human rights, all these proposals posses guarantee of execution within human soul. On the contrary whatever Europeans say are proposals which lack guarantee of their being implemented, Allameh Dr. Iqbal Lahori (RA) says as follows:

"The humanity today, is in need of a spiritual interpretation of world. The first thing, which is required by men, is that world should be given a spiritual and meaningful interpretation instead of a materialistic one, i.e. first thing which has resulted in men's confusion and with the result any thinking or ideology in the form of real faith can't be planted within men's soul—is materialism and materialistic interpretation of world. That world and whatever therein is consists of matter, world is deaf, dumb and blind; world is silly and stupid; it's without any purpose; it doesn't understand truth and falsehood; nothing in world has a goal and we have been created in vain."

In Dr. Iqbal's opinion it's this thinking which has destroyed the spirit of human civilization and is still destroying. First thing which is required by men

cultural struggle is most crucial, because once people are deprived of their basic ideology beliefs, and culture, then the pagans become victorious without firing a single bullet and waging a single military operation. Islam as God's Last Monotheistic Message still possess, the Holy Qur'an that had still remained completely unchanged[1] in its original form unlike earlier divine scriptures revealed to other divine messengers, together with the most authentic traditions of the Holy Prophet (SAW) and his Ahl al-Bayt (AS) who lived for a period of 250 years after his sad demise. However it's just a matter of its true and sincere implementation in our daily lives. Sometimes it happens that a society possesses theoretical knowledge and fundamental beliefs of its religion nevertheless the circumstances are such that it's practical implementation is not possible due to many complex factors of modern living in high-tech societies.

---

is spiritual interpretation of world as has been described by the Holy Qur'an as follows:

"Deemed ye then that We had created you for naught, and that ye would not be returned unto Us?

—The Holy Qur'an (23:115).

In accordance with the Last Holy Scripture, nothing of this world is nonsense. The world exists upon justice and righteousness. It's seer, listener, wise, and aware as the following verse of the Holy Qur'an explains: ***"God! There is no God save Him, the Alive, the Eternal. Neither slumber nor sleep overtaketh Him."***

—The Holy Qur'an (2:255).

—Truth and Falsehood & Renaissance of Islamic Thought by Martyr Ayatollah Motheri (RA). [Tr]

1. It's is common belief among all Shi'i and Sunni scholars that any sort of deviations has not been done in the Holy Qur'an which is in our hands and it's the same that was revealed to the Holy Prophet (SAW) and nothing has been added or deleted from its original text. Further if all of worlds most powerful tyrants, deviated thinkers, politicians, and warriors would join hands, they would not be able to silence its celestial illumination since God has assumed it's absolute protection in his hands—from annihilation, destruction, and safeguarding from all sorts of fallacious reasoning by whispering enemies. Refer to the verse (15:9): ***"Lo! We even We reveal the Reminder, and lo! We verily are its Guardians."*** [Tr]

The role of patience has been emphasized a lot in the Holy Qur'an and the Holy Prophet's (SAW) and Ahl al-Bayt's (AS) most authentic traditions. Also patience has been described like honey which is sweet but bitter, it's practicing is rather difficult but God always helps those who try to practice it. In a nutshell the position of patience in the complex of Islam is responsible for fulfillment of all aspirations, and all short term and long term goals whether individual or social. In the Persian poetry lots of beautiful verses have been complied in describing the importance of the patience. Here we would present the following few examples like a drop from the infinite ocean of Persian literature:[1]

Sayyid Rohullah Mosavi has translated Imam's (AS) verses about the patience in the Persian as follows:

"Agar pursi tu az hale nihanam,

Choo kohe sabri az ranje jahanam.

Chira az darde khud goyam ke beenam,

Aduv, shad ast wa ghamgeen dostanam."

English Translation:

"If you ask about my inner sorrows,

Like a mountain of patience, in facing world's sorrows.

Why should I speak about my hidden pains,

To make my enemies happy & friends sad."

And the following:

"Goyand sang l'al shaved der maghame sabr,

---

[1] Refer to *Mithlha wa Mithlwaraha der Nahj al-Blagheh* by Fatimeh Ahmadi. [Tr]

A'ari shaved, walik beh khune jigar shaved."

—Hafiz Shirazi

English Translation:

"It's said that a stone turns into ruby due to patience,

Yes, it does so, but only through drinking his own lever's blood."

And another one:

"Sad hazara kimya haq a'afrid,

Kimyai hamchoon sabr adam nadeed.

Sabr karden jane tasbeehate tust,

Sabr kun ke a'an ast tasbeeh drust.

Heech tasbeehi nadarad a'an daraj,

Sabr kun al-sabr mafateeh al-faraj."

English Translation:

"God has created one thousand alchemies,

Men have not seen an alchemy like patience.

Practicing patience is the soul of Your praises,

Be patient since it's the correct praise.

None of the praises have such quick result,

Be patient because it's the key of divine help."

—Molana Romi

And the following:

"Yousuf husani wa ein a'alm choo chah,

Vein rasan, sabr ast bar amrillah."

English Translation:

"Joseph the handsome; and this world is like a well,

That rope—is the patience by God's command."

—Molana Romi.

Following is a sermon regarding the importance of patience in the Path of Eloquence *(Nahj al-Balagheh)* of Imam Ali (AS):

"When God witnessed their patience in resisting tortures and hardships, which were inflicted upon them, because of their love for Him and in their following path of truth; he opened over them gates of divine assistance in the midst of those difficult bottlenecks of misfortunes. The deprived of yesterday after that find them as rulers, their glory, fame, and prestige reached to the point that which had never been seen in their best dreams."[1]

Now the best manifestation of above sermon of Commander of Faithful, Imam Ali (AS) could be example of the Supreme Leader of Islamic Republic of Iran, Grand Ayatollah Sayyid Ali Khamenei. He was exiled by Pahlavi regime in Iranshahr (Sistan and Baluchestan Province)—a town with worst climatic conditions in southeast of Iran—before the victory of Islamic Revolution. Today, after 37 years or so, by the divine help he is the Supreme Leader of I.R. Iran and may God prolong his life until the appearance of the Lord of Age Imam al-Mehdi (AF) accompanied by the Holy Prophet Jesus Christ (AS).

---

[1] Sermon # 234, Peak of Eloquence, *(Nahj al-Blagheh)*

Further, God has clearly reminded us that Islam is the greatest source of power and it can do wonders, that power of faith is far mightier than that of superpowers. The Holy Qur'an has stated as follows:

"God has promised such of you as believe and do good works that He will, surely make them to succeed (the present rulers) in the earth, even as He caused those who were before them to succeed (others); and that He will surely establish for them their religion which He hath approved for them, and will them in exchange safety after their fear. They serve Me. They ascribe nothing as partner unto Me. Those who disbelieve henceforth, they are the miscreants. Establish worship and pay the poor due and obey the messenger, that haply ye may find mercy. Think not that the disbelievers can escape in the land. Fire will be their home—a hapless journey's end."

—The Holy Qur'an (24:55-57).

The book consists of five chapters covering various aspects of patience and its direct relationship with the final victory: Importance of Patience, Importance of Patience in Traditions, Patience in Islamic Codices, The Fields of Patience, Historical Examples, and Advantages and Effects of Patience. I have tried to be loyal to the Persian text with best of my abilities. The notes added by the translator have been indicated by [Tr]. I am sincerely indebted to Dr. Muhammad Jowad al-Ansari, Detroit, Michigan for his prompt help in the translation of Arabic texts. Of course special thanks are due to very skilled and professional Author House Publishing team namely: Rowella Alvaro and Allen Endrina for their sincere cooperation and diligence in publishing the book in an excellent manner. Although I have tried my best to make its translation as simple as possible, nevertheless, it's obvious that this translation won't be without mistakes, errors, and omissions for which I apologize to my readers in advance and sincerely welcome their valuable suggestions and comments. May God, bless all those who have contributed in completion of this work, its translator, publisher, readers, with The Holy Prophet's (SAW) intercession on the Day of Judgment! Amen.

With God's blessing since the Islamic Revolution of Iran under the leadership of Imam Khomeini (RA), in 1979, the curiosity to learn and understand the pure and true Islam has already overwhelmed Islamic as well as non-Islamic world. People do have access to the Holy Qur'an's various English translations but it needs to be complimented with the Holy Prophet's (SAW) Ahl al-Bayt's (AS) learning, knowledge, and most authentic traditions. There is a special need for translating them from Arabic/Persian into English, for the researchers, intellectuals, and truth seekers living in the United States of America and other western English speaking countries.

Sayyid Hussein Alamdar,
Ahl al-Bayt (AS) Islamic Cultural Services (AICS) of USA.
alamdar_zaidi2000@yahoo.com
www.sayyidalamdar.com
www.amazon.com/author/sayyidalamdar
Rabi Al-Awaal 1437 A.H, Azar 24, 1394, December 15, 2015

2. Biography of Grand Ayatollah Sayyid Ali Khamenei

He was born in the year 1939 in the holy city of Mashad in Khorasan province, Northeastern Iran. Both his parents belonged to religious scholarly families and he spent his childhood years in a spiritual atmosphere. He successfully completed his theological studies at the famous Islamic Seminary of Qum in the year 1964 and subsequently pursued religious studies at the Theological Academy at Mashad till the year 1968. During the deposed Pahlavi regime he was one of the most beloved and bright pupil of Imam Khomeini (RA), and was considered to be one of the most prominent and trusted leaders of the Islamic movement, which entered into a new critical phase on 5th. of June 1963 (15th of Khordad, 1342), after Imam Khomeini's (RA) historical stand against the ex-Shah's regime. During this struggle he was repeatedly arrested and spent three years in prison between 1964 and 1978. Later he was exiled for almost a year to a place with one of worst climatic conditions.

In 1978, upon his return from exile and at the height of revolutionary struggle of Iranian Muslims, together with a few of his close associates he led the struggle of people in Khorasan. Later in the same year when Imam Khomeini (RA) headed the Islamic revolutionary movement from Naples Le Chateau at Paris, France, he was selected to be a member of the Revolutionary Council. After the down fall of monarchy and formation of revolutionary government, he was entrusted with responsibility of representing Revolutionary Council of Army. He also served as deputy for revolutionary affairs at the Ministry of Defense, and later on was appointed as Commander of Islamic Revolutionary Guards Corps (IRGC). He was also chosen to lead Friday Congregational Prayers in Tehran, by the Leader of Islamic Revolution, Imam Khomeini (RA), and was elected to the first Islamic Consultative Assembly, as representative of Tehran in 1980. After the formation of Supreme Defense Council, he was nominated to be representative of the Leader of Revolution. He was one of the founding members of Islamic Republic Party in Iran and was appointed as its first Secretary-General.

He was victim of an un-successful assassination attempt on 27 June 1981. His speech at Consultative Assembly was instrumental in Bani Sadr's dismissal from the presidency of Islamic Republic of Iran, and while addressing congregation after leading prayer in a mosque in Tehran, a time bomb exploded nearby, seriously injuring his hand, face, and chest. He was immediately rushed to the hospital by devoted people of Tehran and miraculously survived. His right hand however is still not functioning properly. In 1981, following Muhammad Ali Rajaei's martyrdom, second President of Islamic Republic of Iran, he become a candidate, and was elected as President of Islamic Republic of Iran with 95 % of votes cast in his favor by Iranian people (the total number of votes was 16,847,717). He was reelected as President in 1985 for a second term. He also headed Supreme Council for Cultural Revolution. During imposed war, he visited various fronts, and continuously inspected front lines in order to boost the morale of Islamic Combatants and to give advise on organizational matters. After the sad demise of Imam Khomeini (RA), Leader of the Islamic Revolution, the Assembly of Experts *(Majlis-e-Khubregan)* selected him as the next Supreme Leader of Islamic Republic of Iran on June 4, 1989.

He has a good command of Persian, Arabic, Azeri, and Turkish languages as well as is also acquainted with English. Grand Ayatollah Khamenei is an eminent scholar and religious authority in the Islamic jurisprudence and is one of the most eloquent orators in the Islamic world at present. In addition to writings, he has a sense of appreciation for literary and poetic work. He has translated numerous books on Islam and history. His translations include Future of Islamic Lands, An Indictment against Western Civilization, and Imam Hasan's (AS) Peace Treaty. From his writings one may mention: The Role of Muslims in the Independence Struggle of India, General Pattern of Islamic Thoughts in the Holy Qur'an, Importance of Patience and Prayers, Understanding Islam Properly, Imam Sadiq's (AS) Life, A 250 years Old Human Being, and a collection of lectures about the Vicegerency *(Vilayat)*. He was also a co-writer of famous pamphlet: Our Positions, which helped political, social, and philosophical advancement of Islamic Republic Party. Other contributors were Martyr Ayatollah Beheshti, Martyr Hujjatul Islam Dr. Bahonar, and Ayatollah Hashemi Rafsanjani.

Chapter-3: Importance of Patience

Patience is considered to be one of the best known terms in Islam. In Islamic literature, this phrase occurs with frequency in proportion to different occasions and in various fields with a tone of encouragement, discussion of rewards, praise, and explanation about its importance. It's therefore natural that Muslims become familiar with its meaning, understand this special phrase, and try to breed this virtue within themselves with best of their abilities. Unfortunately, alteration or tampering, which is a very common calamity especially for Islamic phrases, has not left this term untouched, and it could be said that up to a large extent its form, matter, and substance have been completely metamorphosed.

3.1. Common Understanding of Patience

Normally, patience is defined as tolerance of unpleasant circumstances, this definition to a larger extent is intermingled with ambiguities, justifications, opposing statements, and conflicts. For an oppressed and unintelligent society steeped in to corruption and decadence, patience as defined above will become biggest tool and pattern for oppressors and corruptors for maintaining the status quo, through it in a state of backwardness. When poor and backward nations exposed to all kinds of problems and misery, oppressed masses crushed under brute oppression, societies faced with moral corruption, poverty and human suffering, and any individual or group trapped in a cesspool of misfortune and calamities are told to be patient–the first result will be taking of that bitter and fatal dose, i.e. to continue suffering, and not to overthrow the existing state of oppression.

Not only will they not mobilize themselves to overthrow existing undesirable state of oppression, but on the contrary keeping in mind supposed rewards for remaining indifferent and naive they would feel happy and content to the extent that they would regard such behavior as tantamount to accomplishment of a grand victory. It's obvious that prevalence of such a mentality in that society up to a large extent will be to the advantage of class of exploiters and oppressors, and to further detriment of deprived and oppressed masses. Unfortunately, this wrong interpretation together with its disastrous results presently constitutes the sorry state of affairs in Islamic societies. Any other interpretation for free and unprejudiced minds is quite logical and acceptable, but for those accustomed to its false interpretation even serious endeavors would not produce any fruitful results. When detailed studies of the Holy Qur'an's verses and authentic narrations about the patience are conducted, grief and surprise for this deviation becomes relatively intense.

3.2. Overall Views about Patience

If meanings of patience are interpreted in the light of clear, explicit, and definite the Holy Qur'an's verses as well as in accordance with authentic traditions reported from the Holy Prophet (SAW) and Impeccable Imams (AS), then result derived would be completely opposite to current common understanding of the term. The above interpretation transforms patience into a lever capable of removing with ease, the heaviest obstacles and solving biggest problems with one hundred percent positive results. Thus, for an unfortunate society, patience is key to prosperity and blessings, while on the other hand it will be a strong obstacle to be reckoned with for troublemakers and mischief mongers. In order to appreciate exactly true meanings of patience and its relevant fields, the best methodology is to resort to the Holy Qur'an and authentic traditions. A thorough investigation would enable us to reach a clear and decisive judgment. More than seventy verses of the Holy Qur'an, deal with patience, glorifying the term and praising those who possess this virtue. The Holy Qur'an describes in detail to possess this virtue, relevant results derived, and the circumstances where one could count on this characteristic.

For present discussion, we will not resort to the Holy Qur'an's verses regarding patience, rather it will suffice our discussion to review the authentic traditions, and accordingly derive inferences and conclusions because of the following reasons. Firstly, precise and detailed interpretation of the Holy Qur'an's verses regarding patience would mean a wide discussion, which requires a lot of patience, energy and time.[1] Secondly, in order to try to compensate for negligence shown towards the authentic traditions which were narrated by Impeccable Imams (AS), our discussion will be based upon them. Absence of use of authentic traditions is clearly felt in the current Islamic research and published Islamic literature.

3.3. Summary of Meanings of Patience

On the basis of traditions, patience is defined as resistance shown by men on the road towards perfection against mischief, corruption, and degradation. Which can be compared to the example of a mountaineer who in order to reach the peak, has to face internal as well as external obstacles or barriers. The internal obstacles are within his inner self, while external ones are outside beyond his control. Each of them in their own ways interfere with his climbing efforts. Internal obstacles such as love for comfort as well as fear, despair, and different types of similar passions, try to stop him while feeling of indecisiveness in many forms tries to kill his determination for climbing. On the other hand external barriers such as stones, rocks, wolves, thieves, and thorns etc retard his progress. Someone who is faced with these kinds of barriers will have options to either drop his journey on this road which is full of dangers and hardships, or to go ahead by offering resistance against them, and overcoming each barrier with his power of determination—here the second case is defined as patience.

During his limited span of life in this world, a human being between his birth and death is a traveler on the road towards his final

[1] A point in contrast to those who have totally disregarded the Holy Qur'an for understanding of principles and branches of Islam, and depend upon traditions however weak as the only source of religion.

destination. He has been fundamentally created to endeavor as much as possible to bring himself close to his final destination. All duties and responsibilities which have been assigned to men's shoulders are necessary means and ways to bring him closer to that target. The primary aim of divine religions and great prophets was to build an Islamic society providing a suitable field in which human beings could travel, ultimately reaching their desired goals. In a nutshell that aim could be defined as striving for perfection and exaltation of human beings. In other words it's opening of fountainheads of talents of his inner self, his acquiring of superior and noble characteristics overrides animalistic characteristics or lower qualities.

Of course this path is a difficult one full of troubles and plenty of barriers. Each of these barriers alone is sufficient to deter climber from continuing his journey towards the peak of perfection and exaltedness. The inner negative forces inside climber of un weighed evil passions, coupled with external forces such as troublesome state of affairs of real world, produce a series of obstacles of thorns, rocks, etc in his path. Patience means to be able to stand up against all those obstacles and to conquer them with determination and enthusiasm. Therefore, as was mentioned earlier, all Islamic obligations whether individual or collective (social) are means and steps needed to approach that goal of perfection. For a person on a journey towards a distant city traveling through deserts, passing of each habitation that lies in his path means that his journey is progressing or he is getting closer to his final destination. Of course these intermediate aims or targets themselves are preliminaries of path towards reaching real and final destination. Therefore each step taken, although a means for accomplishing ultimate aim, is nevertheless in itself a multidimensional accomplishment and may be regarded as something closer to the final objective.

The summary of this discussion is that to reach each of these goals and destinations, basic condition is possession of patience and ability to utilize this sharp and decisive weapon. Just as road towards accomplishment of ultimate goal of perfection is full of obstacles, similarly paths of Muslims fulfilling their Islamic duties and responsibilities are also full of these obstacles. These paths are a means for reaching the final destination. There are infinite internal and external obstacles scattered on these roads. On one hand, depressing internal feelings of laziness, indifference, selfishness, self-praise, pride, greed, and improper sexual desires, as well as various harmful desires of comfort, wealth, fame, etc, haunt the traveler. While on the other hand unfavorable conditions, interruptions, and situations forced or superimposed upon people because of social set up of ruling regimes confront him. Each one of above in a way discourages him from carrying out his constructive duties, which either could be individual duties such as offering prayers, or other social obligations like his efforts for proclamation of truth. The thing which would enable and guarantee discharge of each duty, undertaking of each step, proceeding on each road, and accomplishing of each result—is the resistance offered by men against these obstacles. Thus the power which enables him to proceed through these barriers—is defined as patience.

Chapter-4: Importance of Patience in Traditions

According to a few traditions selected from a collection describing importance of patience in Islam and other divine religions, it may be summarized that it has been recommended by all divine prophets and righteous leaders to their successors and followers. Let us consider the example of a kind father or a compassionate teacher who has spent a life full of efforts and resistance, and had suffered pains, tortures, and deprivations for the sake of his goals. At last moments of his life, all struggles which provided purpose and direction to his life are now nearing an end, and his goals are still cherished. What will be his last advice for his successors, who in his opinion will follow the struggle and keep movement alive through taking other giant steps to carry this heavy load closer to final destination?

It will be nothing other than extraction and summary of all theoretical and practical experiences and possessions acquired by him in his life span. All those things which must be said in his last moments, if he could manage to put them into one sentence, will be like a capsule consisting of all precious accomplishments and practical know how acquired by him in the form of guidelines designed for a trainee. He will hand this over to his successor and follower, which in reality means transformation of final designation of his life to the person after him. This mission being accomplished, he leaves this world after making due preparations. Last parting recommendations of divine prophets, pious, righteous, martyrs and strugglers in God's way for their followers and builders of divine society has always been to emphasize regarding practicing patience. Now let us pay our attention towards the following two traditions:

4.1. First Narration

Abu Hamza Thomali, one of the famous and sincere followers of the Holy Prophet's (SAW) Ahl al-Bayt (AS) and a principal member of righteous Shi'i movement quotes from his leader and teacher—Imam Muhammad al-Baqir (AS), as follows:

"When the last moments of his life arrived, my father Ali ibn al-Husain (AS) held me close to his chest and said: 'My son I recommend to you what my father, Imam al-Husain (AS) recommended to me at last moments of his life, my son stand for truth even if it's bitter.'"

—Al-Kafi, v. 2

Imam Mohammad al-Baqir (AS) is the vicegerent and successor of his father Ali ibn al-Husain—Zain al-A'abedin (AS), inheritor of the heavy burden of trust, and responsible for continuation of struggle and movement of his father, exactly in the same manner that Imam Ali ibn al-Husain (AS) was responsible for continuation of the movement left by his father Imam al-Husain ibn Ali (AS)—the Martyr of Karbala. Each personality from the Holy Prophet's (SAW) household was responsible for continuation of divine mission of his predecessor, and all of them collectively were upholders of divine mission of God's last prophet. All of them were created from a single source of energy (light) and seekers of one direction and one aim: ***"My son I recommend you what my father recommended me at last moment of his life."***

We all know how and where last moments of Imam al-Husain ibn Ali's (AS) life were spent. He was in the midst of most tragic catastrophes on the Day of A'ashura—10th. of Muharram 61 Hijri, 680 AD. Pains, torture, and tragedy dominated the bloody state of affairs in the plain of Karbala. In spite of the fact that he was completely encircled by his bloodthirsty enemies, Imam al-Husain ibn Ali (AS) took advantage of a short opportunity to go back to his camp before starting his final attack. After having a brief meeting with members of his household who in their own ways were carriers of his mission, he held a short but sufficient, effective, and very important discussion with his vicegerent and successor—Imam Ali ibn al-Husain (AS). These kinds of discussions in simple language may be called farewell meetings. But it must be understood that a pious leader (imam) is far above sentimental passions, and that during last opportunity of his life, he would only open his lips for personal, private, and sentimental affairs, instead of discussing the most important issues of his mission. Whatever reports which remain regarding other great pious leaders, Impeccable Imams (AS) that has reached us certify the same thing.[1]

He knew at that sensitive moment that heavy burden of trust for which he had struggled since the beginning of his leadership had also been endured by the founder of revolution, the Holy Prophet (SAW), the Commander of Faithful, Imam Ali (AS), and Imam al-Hasan (AS). All of them had suffered different kinds of pains and were subjected to severe hardships for following that path, the trust would now be handed over to the next person. The powerful arms and steadfast steps of his vicegerent would be assigned the responsibility to carry that burden of trust forward. Therefore he had come to advice him about most important issues of his mission. What was this important and cherished advice? Now Imam Ali ibn al-Husain (AS) who found himself more or less under conditions similar to his father's time, explained key issues to his son and vicegerent, and offered recommendations accordingly. He also emphasized that earlier, his father Imam Husain ibn Ali (AS) had been similarly instructed by his father Imam Ali (AS) that is what his father has exactly recommended to him. This advice has continuously been emphasized since it was first given by the Commander of Faithful, Imam Ali (AS) to the next Imam-designate and onward through all successive Impeccable Imams (AS) by their predecessors. What was that recommendation? The outcome and summation of that advice was patience—***"My son stand for truth even if its bitter."***

"My son! Stand for the truth and be patient, even if it's bitter and inconvenient." Or in other words, on the road of truth one should

---

1. Among the books of traditions we may observe the wills of the Commander of Faithful Imam Ali (AS), Imam al-Hasan (AS), Imam al-Sadiq (AS), and other leaders which proves the same point.

never give up, and never be frustrated by obstacles. Once you know and recognize the path of truth—you must support it all the way. All hardships, bitterness, failures, and inconveniencies should be borne patiently to continue the journey forward. It's obvious that confrontation of truth and falsehood is full of hardship, bitterness, inconvenience, and one should not expect this path to be like a bed of roses. All these inconveniencies and hardships should be resisted with patience for the sake of truth. This was the last will of the Commander of Faithful, Imam Ali (AS) given to Imam al-Hasan (AS), and subsequently it was given to all successive Imams (AS) by their predecessors. Also, we have witnessed that the Commander of Faithful, Imam Ali (AS) himself, and all righteous Impeccable Imams (AS) after him, had actually followed that will. All of them till the last moment of their lives defended truth accepting all consequences, even at the cost of their lives—martyrdom. Their lives in practicing patience for God's pleasure, were indeed manifestations of the following Arabic couplet:

"I practiced patience in my life to the highest level,

Whereby even patience itself bears witness that,

In tolerating things even bitter than patience,

I remained steadfast and patient."

Therefore, for the importance of patience it's found, that all Impeccable Imams (AS) from the Holy Prophet's (SAW) Ahl al-Bayt (AS) have enjoined this priceless jewel and noble inheritance in their wills for their successors at the very last moment of their lives.

4.2. Second Narration

From Imam al-Rida's (AS) jurisprudence we narrate the divine prophet's wills as follows:

"Be patient for the truth even if it's bitter."

—Bihar al-Anwar

Imam al-Rida's (AS) jurisprudence *(fiqh)* is a famous book attributed to eighth Imam Ali ibn Musa al-Rida (AS), a portion of which deals with legal affairs in Islam. In other words these issues may be termed as jurisprudence. This term partly deals with the interpretation of the Holy Qur'an, and authentic traditions but major portion of book covers ways and means and overall issues related to Islamic learning. It's this second part which constitutes complete and comprehensive portion of the term of jurisprudence. The above mentioned book contains the following meaningful narration[1] which could be interpreted and expounded as follows:

We narrate this important narration, which is inheritance and memory of our noble family left by our fathers and their ancestors, who left this last will for us, and in turn we willed it to our successors. The will of all divine prophets for their vicegerents, inheritors, trustees, flag carriers of divine movements, and students of divine school of thought was: ***"Stand for the truth and be patient even if it's bitter and inconvenient."*** This is exactly the same sentence spoken by the Commander of Faithful, Imam Ali (AS) without the least variation. Perhaps this short but meaningful sentence left by divine prophets and their vicegerents, could be best example for showing importance of patience. Therefore, on the basis of above two narrations, we may define patience, as the will enjoined by divine prophets and Impeccable Imams (AS) on their inheritors and disciples. It's quite explicit that this Islamic characteristic has so much weight, importance, and influence, in the complex structure of divine religion of Islam that all divine prophets had included it in their testaments.

---

1. Late Muhaddis Nouri (RA), who was a most exalted and learned scholar of his time in his book: *Mustadrek al-Wasail* had presented numerous logical convincing arguments, testifying the authenticity of the above issues. Nouri's work is very interesting for the learned scholars in the field of traditions.

Chapter-5: Patience in Islamic Codices

Faith may be defined as something which consists of ethics, legal rights, and public instructions. The same is the case for any other, constructive social school or organization. We may therefore classify faith into following:

1. The basis for understanding of men and world. This is known as world-view.

2. On the basis of these principles, overall direction for the movement and human action—ideology.

3. Within these boundaries, guidelines or regulations for relationship of men with God, self, fellow human beings, and other creatures.

4. A series of moral guidelines for maintaining required necessary momentum or endeavor for achieving perfection or exaltedness, and accomplishing success in various fields of life.

Of course, this vast complex, includes personal matters related to personal interests of individuals, as well as social matters pertaining to various large groups of humanity, and affairs concerning these groups and Islamic community. Let us see in the above complex of faith, what is influence and key roll played by patience. In other words, a person sincerely committed to religion will act as follows:

1. He must believe in all religious principles.

2. He must obey all religious regulations.

3. He must be familiar with special clauses dealing with ethics.

If one fulfills all of the above three in his conduct he could then rightly be called a true believer. We will now examine role played by patience in the life of a believer in following the religion in true sense. In a geometrical figure which consists of lines and angles, each point, arc and semi circle creates a special effect. Let us see what influence and role is played by patience in geometrical figure representing faith of a true believer. Let us consider example of an automobile which is supposed to move someone together with his house-hold belongings to a certain location. After passing through various streets, this automobile finally reaches desired final destination. What is responsible for moving this automobile? Is it engine?

What thing is responsible for providing this strength or power to engine? Of course, it's gasoline. Therefore, in the life of a believer, patience may be compared to engine or gasoline which gives life and strength to that engine. Without patience, truth and steadfast logic of exalted school of religion would not have been understood. Divine learning and revelations of this school which blessed humanity would have lost its color with the passage of time. Ultimate hope of victory of truth over falsehood, which provides fresh life-giving blood for powerful hands and steadfast steps of believers, would have been silenced. And laws and guidelines of religion which control and check human tendencies of transgression would have become inactive.

Heroic field of valor and martyrdom for the sake of God and religion would have been converted into graveyards of ideologies. The international congress of Hajj would have remained empty. The humming, sensational and confidential communications of burning lovers (believers) in the middle of night, with their beloved (God) would have been silenced, beautiful scene of great struggle with self namely: fasting and self restriction would have lost its charms. Arteries of economy of Islamic state would have dried up, and charity and alms-giving for God's pleasure would have been ignored. Without patience all higher educational and ethical values of Islam—piety, trust, and righteousness would have been forgotten, and in essence each parameter of religion which requires action and efforts, would have remained deprived of them. Because religion requires practice which is not possible without patience. Therefore, what provides life-giving fresh blood to this giant complex, or what provides motion to this train is nothing else but patience. With above discussion, substance and meaning of this divine inspiration could be clearly understood. According to some documented narrations related to Impeccable Imams (AS), importance of patience has been defined as follows:

"Patience in faith is like a head to a body."

Head of a person holds most critical importance as far as life is concerned. One may tolerate absence of different parts in human body such as hands, feet, eyes, ears etc, but if the head which is controlling room for whole nervous system, does not exist or is crippled, then all parts and systems of the body will become crippled. Body may remain alive, but in reality it will not be different than a dead body. Sometimes, it may be that a part of body may perform an outstanding task, may be the fist, a powerful hand, fingers, or eyes of a person might conduct excellent performance in discharging many duties, but all that is accomplished because of presence of head. Patience holds similar importance in the structure of religion.

Without patience existence of Monotheism, prophet-hood, and prophetic mission wouldn't have been possible and produced any fruits. Prophet hood and prophetic mission would not have produced any fruits. Rights of deprived people could not have been obtained from the tyrants, and prayers, fasting, and other rituals would also have been meaningless. Therefore, it's patience which fulfills all aspirations of religion and humanity. If at the very beginning of Islam, if the Holy Prophet (SAW) would have not offered resistance against all that severe opposition, for the sake of truth, of course, the slogan: ***There is no god but God***, would have been suffocated within the boundary walls of his home at its very inception. What kept Islam alive and intact was patience.

Had God's pious people and great divine prophets not remained patient against opposition and obstacles in their path, today there would not have been left any trace and influence of Monotheism. Single factor responsible for keeping alive system of Monotheism, since very beginning of human creation has been patience, which has been flag carrier for this heavenly ideology until today, and will continue to do the same till the Day of Judgment. Most logical ideas and sayings of human beings, if not accompanied by patience practiced by their founders, would have dried off in their throats and tongues. They would have disappeared in turbulent waves of the ocean of history forever. It's therefore quite clear that patience holds similar relationship with religious body, as the position of head relative to a human body. The Commander of Faithful, Imam Ali (AS) in his sermon *Qaseyeh* explains the victory of deprived of history over tyrants and success of their noble ideas as follows:

"When God witnessed their patience in resisting tortures and hardships, which were inflicted upon them, because of their love for Him and following the path of truth, He opened over them gates of divine assistance in the midst of those difficult bottlenecks of misfortunes. The deprived of yesterday[1] after they find themselves as rulers and governors. Their glory, fame, prestige, reached to a point, which had never been imagined in their best of dreams."

—Nahj al-Balagheh, Sermon # 234.

---

[1] The present book is based on the lectures of Grand Ayatollah Khamenei at a Mashad Mosque 40 years ago as mentioned in the introduction. Now, in retrospect, the best manifestation of the above sermon of the Commander of the Faithful, Imam Ali (AS) could be, victory of the Islamic Revolution on February 11th, 1979. In an article a few years ago written by Dr. Hasan Ghafoorifard, the then Head of the Physical Education Organization in a Sports Magazine, it was mentioned that Grand Ayatollah Khamenei was confined in Iranshahr (Sistan and Boluchistan Province), a town with the worst climatic conditions in the Southeast of Iran, before the victory of Islamic Revolution. Today, by the Grace of God he is the Supreme Leader of I.R. Iran. The honor and fame awarded to him and to all other leaders now, who were imprisoned under the Pahlavi regime is a clear manifestation of above sermon. [Tr]

This is a tradition of history, which will never be changed till the very end, as the laws of God are constant, irrespective of time. Therefore, after above detailed explanation one could describe in a nutshell position of patience in the complex of Islam as follows:

Patience is responsible for fulfillment of all aspirations, and all short term and long term goals whether individual or social.

Chapter-6: Fields of Patience

As explained in earlier chapters of this book, one may define patience as resistance offered by men on the road towards perfection against forces of mischief, corruption, and degradation. Now let us recognize fields of patience, where its practice is most crucial. Of course, we would like to examine the domain of patience, in accordance with texts of Islamic narrations and the Holy Qur'an, where, practicing patience has been promised with plenty of rewards in this world as well as in the hereafter. There is no doubt, that an ignorant soldier or a mercenary fighting in battlefield against bearers of glad tidings of truth and justice, even loosing his life for the sake of orders issued by his master; or a tyrant, hoarder of wealth, and holder of an important position, standing against truth for the sake of power, wealth, and position; or various sections or special groups offering resistance for the sake of their vested interests or other reasons—are in fact not practicing patience for the sake of human ideals but instead of opposing truth. On the surface all these cases show practicing of patience, but this is quite opposite than patience practiced by pious individuals on the road of perfection for God's pleasure. Of course as far as lexical meaning of term patience is concerned both share it equally.

In all such situations, patience has not been practiced for accomplishing human perfection and ideals, rather for their suppression. Here resistance was not offered against forces of mischief, corruption and degradation, but instead it was offered to destroy shining manifestations of human perfection. Therefore, this domain of patience is not the domain as defined in authentic traditions and the Holy Qur'an. It could therefore be concluded that patience may be defined as a means of achieving perfection, excellence, and exaltedness, where men endeavors and makes sincere efforts for ultimate goal of creation, to become a real servant of God. His personality ultimately becomes manifestation of all hidden potential of human talents and characteristics, or in other words achieving the status of a perfect human being *(insan-e-kamil).* At this stage all internal and external obstacles explained in detail earlier, which compliment each other, and in any case are manifestations of Satanic tactics, are resisted by him, on his forward journey. On this road all kinds of dangers, headaches, and obstacles await the traveler, opposition provided by them varies in proportion to traveler's location, movement, and duties. Sometimes for discharging a duty one is confronted with a direct obstacle, while at other times one is confronted with an indirect barrier in his path.

For a mountain climber, trying to scale the highest peaks, confrontation with rocks, thorns, thieves and wolves, all are tantamount to a negative force interfering with his ascent. But sometimes a beautiful scene, a comfortable soft bed, and a shaky companion are also negative forces of another sort, which force climber to terminate his ascent. Still, at other times it could be his own sickness, or he has to take care of some sick companions, or might be confronted with some other mishap, which ultimately forces him to terminate his expedition. This last case may be regarded as an indirect obstacle in his path. The above analogy of mountain climbing is also true for the journey of men on the road of perfection. He is confronted with three kinds of obstacles in this journey. If compulsory duties and obligations of religion may be considered as instruments and steps required for forward march on the road of perfection, forbidden acts of religion may be regarded as diversion from straight path. And if unforeseen bitter happenings of life at the time of restlessness and instability are considered responsible for slowing down and ultimately cutting short his journey, then obstacles and opposing motives could also divided into following three categories:

1. Desires and passions which are responsible for negligence of compulsory religious obligations.

2. Desires and tendencies which encourage a human being to indulge into forbidden sinful acts.

3. Unforeseen, unhappy happenings which result in breaking his courage and steadfastness.

Patience means resistance against all three types of barriers, and providing moral courage and necessary momentum for traveler to continue his forward journey on the road of perfection. It offers resistance against those desires and tendencies which discourage a human being from performing compulsory obligations, resists desires for indulging into sinful forbidden acts, and provides zeal and strength to be able to tolerate unforeseen and unhappy occurrences, which threaten to break his determination. With above explanation one may appreciate context of this important narration from the Holy Prophet (SAW) as related by the Commander of the Faithful, Imam Ali (AS) as follows:

The Holy Prophet (SAW) had said: ***"Patience is of three kinds, namely: Patience in tragedies and unpleasant events, patience in performance of compulsory obligations, and patience against sin."*** On all above mentioned occasions, like occurrence of a tragic unfortunate happening resulting in loss of life or wealth or both, a situation requiring performance of compulsory obligations, and an alluring sinful pleasure tempting him to indulge into a forbidden act; a type of patience is required where human being could manifest or display the most superior heroic potential of his hidden exalted qualities. In order that complete understanding of these Islamic specialties related to these three types of patience could be made explicitly clear, we will now discuss all of them in detail as follows:

6.1. Patience in Performance of Obligations—Obedience

All duties and compulsory obligations are accompanied with some headaches and inconveniences, or in other words, they demand some amount of efforts and involvements either positive or negative, which are at odd with easy going and comfort loving nature of human beings. Starting from personal compulsory religious obligations such as prayers and fasting till financial obligations such as *Khums*[1] and *Zakat*[2], and collective social obligations such as Hajj pilgrimage, separation from family and loved ones, sacrificing all comforts and pleasures of life, and sometimes self-sacrifice itself becomes necessary. Of course, all this does not match with easy going and comfort loving nature of a human being. This holds true for all laws of the world whether heavenly or man-made, be they right or wrong. Although in principle law itself has been a necessity and for the same reason it's accepted by mankind, but generally nowhere, it has ever been accepted as something convenient, desirable, and sweet by human beings. The same holds true for most common international laws and regulations, whose benefits and advantages are explicitly clear for everybody, and their violation will result in serious consequences such as is the case with traffic laws.

Passing through a red light results in most horrible accidents sometimes leading to loss of lives. Although everyone is clearly aware about consequences of traffic law violations, but in spite of above it's very common that while awaiting behind a red light, inner human nature is not comfortable and feels inconvenience. Similar is the case for not being able to drive through a short cut route because of a traffic sign, again one feels uncomfortable. Although compulsory religious obligations are based upon inherent human nature, and without exception to meet its genuine demands—in reality, the means and instruments to lead human beings towards perfection and exaltation—but in spite of that it must be said that in practice it requires efforts and difficulties of some sort. For example, in order to perform compulsory daily prayers one has to spend some time, must clean his hands and face before the prayers, and has to meet other preliminary requirements regarding dress and place in accordance with religious guidelines. It's obvious that all of above are in conflict with easy going human nature. During performance of daily prayers, to control thoughts and to achieve peace of heart and mind strictly for prayers, instead of getting preoccupied in worldly affairs other than God, is very important. In order for prayers to be meaningful, and

---

1. One fifth levy, a yearly tax upon one's personal savings after subtracting all the permissible living expanses.

2. Wealth tax to be paid upon certain items.

to be accepted by God, it's very important that gates which allow all external ideas should be thoroughly closed during prayers.[1]

Of course achieving above state of mind and heart requires lots of energy and efforts and is a difficult task. Or fasting, which requires toleration of hunger and thirst for long periods. To resist and struggle against appetite for eating and drinking, to restrain eyes from looking at forbidden things of beauty and resist sexual passions are difficult tasks requiring tremendous amount of resistance. In spite of possessing appetizing food and drinks, to be able to impose voluntary self restrictions, to spent a long hot summer day with empty stomach and dry lips of course, requires a lot of will power and strong determination. Or Hajj pilgrimage for instance, which requires tolerating inconvenience and hardships of a long distance journey, separation from home and relatives, joining groups of unknown companions, and spending money and precious time. If Hajj pilgrimage is done only for the sake of God's pleasure, without

---

1. In his book: Mysteries of Prayers *(Sirr-us-Salat)*, Imam Khomeini (RA) describes the presence of heart, as follows:

"During prayers one must try to completely cut off heart's preoccupation with worldly affairs. If a person is submerged in love and desires of this world, naturally his heart is busy continuously from one involvement to another. Heart behaves like a bird jumping from one branch to another. So far we have this tree of worldly ambitions or desires (hubb-e-duniya) in our heart—it will behave restless. If by struggle, practice, efforts, and thinking about severe consequences and losses, if one could succeed in cutting this tree of worldly ambitions or desires, then the heart will become reposed and peaceful. It will achieve spiritual perfection. At least the more one tries to free himself from worldly charms and temptations the more he succeeds in cutting various branches of that tree in his heart, with the result, presence of heart will be achieved in same proportion." He further explains the term love of this world (hubb-e-duniya). "There are people who do not possess anything at all in this mortal world, but still they could be persons totally submerged in the love of this world. While on the contrary one could be like Prophet Sulaiman bin Dawood (AS)—Solomon son of David, King of Kings and possessing all treasurers of this universe, but at the same time may not be a man of this world—completely detached from the lure of world." [Tr]

any motives of leisure and profit-making, it will also require patience and self-sacrifice. Obligations regarding encouraging whatever is good *(amr bil ma'roof)* and prohibiting whatever is forbidden *(nahi anil munkar)*, as well as struggle striving for truth requires a lot of hardship, sacrifice, tolerance, and patience.

Proclamation of truth in front of forces of falsehood and corruption is most dangerous, unpleasant and bitter act, which is like standing against a tyrant whose unsheathed sword is ready to fall on a proclaimer's head. Or facing enemies who are like savage beasts, the glint of whose electrifying eyes and swords stun the heart and soul of superficial observers. Or, to be able to offer resistance against waves of corruption and diversion of a nation, a class, or mankind as a whole, is the most hardest, dangerous and menacing task. Similar is the case with other Islamic obligations, which are accompanied with headaches, hardships and inconveniencies, but at the same time without exception, all of them are most beneficial, and essential means and guarantees of salvation and prosperity for mankind. Of course, for those who have recognized straight path and have tasted sweetness of walking on difficult road for God's pleasure, and sacred and exalted aims of humanity—all above difficulties are desirable and tolerable. The same prayer for God's most sincere servants, who have tasted sweetness of fervent prayer and His remembrance is something sweeter than honey. The Holy Prophet (SAW) at the time of prayers was so eager and restless that he used to tell Bilal:[1] ***"O! Bilal please recite the call for prayer (adhan) and make my heart and soul peaceful."***

Same struggle for God's sake by self indulgent people without any insight for ultimate consequences is extremely harsh and undesirable, but for someone with a good spiritual insight and power

---

1. He was born in Mecca, the son of an Abyssinian slave called Rabah; in a city of idol-worship, he was tortured for his belief in the one and only God. He was made the first caller to prayer *(mu'azzin)* in Islam by the Holy Prophet (SAW). After the Holy Prophet's (SAW) death Bilal's legs in his grief failed him. He could not climb up steps to make the call to prayer again and died in Syria, probably in the year 644, AD twelve years after the Holy Prophet's (SAW) death. The Holy Prophet (SAW) called Bilal a man of Paradise.

like the Commander of Faithful, Imam Ali (AS), it's sweeter than honey. For him, all inconveniencies and hardships in this struggle result in strengthening his power of resistance and steadfastness. He himself describes about his astonishing state of morale in a sermon of Path of Eloquence *(Nahj al-Balagheh)* as follows:

"Together with the Holy Prophet (SAW) we fought with our own fathers, sons, brothers, and uncles—but all these unpleasant events had least influence upon us—except that it increased our faith to surrender ourselves to God completely, and made hard things tolerable for us."

But in general these difficulties and hardships exist for common people with weaker spiritual insight, and for those who are not possessed with required determination and will power are bitter and undesirable. Now, what should be done regarding these difficulties which exist in discharging of religious obligations? Since offering of daily compulsory prayers is difficult, presence of heart during prayers and chaining roaming and wondering thoughts are even harder. Since fasting, jihad, hajj pilgrimage, charity, encouraging good and forbidding evil and other social obligations require pains and inconveniencies, then all these should be declared as void. Therefore, we should be allowed to live according to the desires of our heart which is full of passions and a spirit which loves ease and comforts of life. It's here that Islam tells us no! Instead patience must be practiced. Patience in obedience must be practiced against those passions which lure heart away from the prayer carpet, mosque and altar, through getting it preoccupied with hundreds of kinds of amusements, and in turn make prayers spiritless and meaningless. Patience must be practiced against these kinds of desires and prayers should be offered completely with presence of heart and concentration, so that they are accepted by God and are fruitful for us. Patience must be offered against those extremist tendencies which tempt us to enjoy eating and drinking on a hot dry day instead of fasting.

Patience must be practiced in confrontation with enemies in battlefield, where danger shows its real and serious face, and where red death with dynamic speed confronts a human being. The pleasures and sweetness of life, memories of children and relatives, and faces of loved ones become incarnated in the eyes, and all profit-oriented business transactions in one way or other attract his attention, and try to make his determination weak and shaky. Resistance should be offered against all these forces. All obstacles and barriers which interfere with forward march must be removed from the road. Patience must be offered against a proud tyrant whose eyes burn with anger and whose transgression and corruption has pushed a nation to the brink of catastrophe. Such a tyrant must be opposed by each responsible individual. In this situation it's a compulsory obligation for everyone to try to overthrow such a despot. Patience should be practiced against the whispers of Satan—who with thousands of colorful deceits will try to close charitable hands by reminding one of personal needs instead of helping others—through inciting desires for material profits, other worldly ambitions, and will ultimately prevent a person from righteous deeds. He will try to emphasize that a lamp in your own home is more important than the candle of mosque's niche *(mehrab)*. Here, patience comes into picture through offering necessary resistance to above desires, to enable one to discharge his financial and religious obligations.

Yes! Patience should be practiced, one should be patient in obedience and fulfillment of these religious commands. Resistance should be offered against Satanic whispers and passions encouraging transgression. Each case where such resistance is offered assumes a special meaning and special importance in proportion to the greatness of that particular situation. At one place, resistance means to be steadfast in facing enemy in battlefield, or it may be confrontation with self, and sometimes it may be struggle to remain indifferent while facing pangs of poverty and other difficulties. Therefore, patience means to be able to offer resistance in all above circumstances. Patience never allows us to surrender with folded hands to be insulted, give up initiative, and become prisoner of events.

6.2. Examples of Patience in Obedience in Infallible Imams' (AS) Lives

Key phrase which has been emphasized a lot in pilgrimage book of Impeccable Imams (AS), is patience. i.e. ***"You! (Imams)***

remained patient, and practiced patience with pleasure for the sake of God. You! Accepted heavy load of carrying the trust, and in spite of all difficulties and hardships, delivered it to its final destination." Truly, responsibility of guiding mankind and explaining them the truth of religion, resisting tyranny, corruption, and transgression during the days of Impeccable Imams (AS), like any other time, was a difficult task requiring a lot of patience and strong determination. If patience practiced by them was such a type that although unhappy about bad conditions of their times—with hearts bleeding for worsening plight of Muslims and Islam they would had confined themselves to safe boundaries of their homes without taking any concrete steps for destruction of evil and betterment of situation in favor of community—then this type of patience would not have been of any special distinction, prestige, and honor. There is nothing special in this kind of inert behavior and anybody could do it easily, of course, this type of conduct is practiced by weak and uncommitted persons. Prominence and glory which distinguish Impeccable Imams' (AS) lives, and special characteristics which may be repeated while reciting salutations as mentioned in pilgrimage book, was their being patient in obedience to God. This is an area in which many ordinary people found themselves helpless, could not tolerate hardships, and therefore failed to achieve that honor and distinction.

6.3. Review of the Holy Qur'an

It would not be out of context to remind here that among tens of verses of the Holy Qur'an regarding patience of those who have been patient, especially there are many verses about the patience in obedience such: ***"O Prophet! Exhort the believers to fight. If there be of you twenty steadfast they shall overcome two hundred, and if there be of you a hundred steadfast they will overcome a thousands of those who disbelieve, because they (the disbelievers) are a folk without intelligence."***

—The Holy Qur'an (8:65).

The above verse emphasizes importance of offering resistance and being steadfast while confronting interior motives within self, which act as obstacles in the path of a soldier facing an enemy in battlefield. Patient people who have been mentioned in above verse are those that neither flashing swords, nor burning eyes of enemies, neither angry face of red death nor memories of friends and children, pleasures and charms of life, stop them in discharging their obligation to engage in bloody hostilities in battlefield. And none of above make a slight dent in their iron will for obeying God. Another verse from the Holy Qur'an regarding importance of patience in obedience is: ***"And when they went into the field against Goliath and his hosts they said: Our Lord! Bestow on us endurance, make our foothold sure, and give us help against the disbelieving folk."***

—The Holy Qur'an (2:250).

Above verse refers to a group of believers who in order to discharge a compulsory obligation have readied themselves to confront an enemy in battlefield. They are asking God to bless them with spirit of endurance and steadfastness in facing obstacles in their path, and with the result bestow upon them fruit of their endurance, that is achieving victory over the enemies (unbelievers). This verse very explicitly explains meanings of patience in obedience. There are many such verses in the Holy Qur'an, and their detailed and comprehensive discussions here is beyond the scope of our present discussion.

6.4. Patience Against Sin

Naturally, human beings are possessed with desires and passions, which encourage as well as discourage them in doing certain acts. In reality these are instruments for performing all actions, efforts, and endeavors by human beings in their live span. These are called instincts such as, love for self, love for children, love for wealth, love for power, sexual desires, and scores of other such attractions and desires. What are the instructions of Islam regarding above natural human instincts? And how human beings are supposed to behave while confronting their natural instincts? Do they have to surrender themselves to these instincts without any limit or condition? Should these passions be suppressed? Or should they be made completely disabled by means of superimposing rigorous self-discipline? According to Islamic view none of above methods are correct treatment. On the contrary under no circumstances, Islam ignores human instincts, rather it considers them useful and something real to be reckoned with. Islam closes paths of transgression and aggression, but on the other hand through utilizing realistic preventive measures, it dissipates perverse energy associated with them. In reality as basic existence of instinct among human beings is a means for continuation of life, as well as for providing essential necessities of life, similarly mutiny, aggression, and transgression of instinctive passions result in catastrophe and misfortune to human life. If instinct of love for self did not exist, continuation of human life would have not been possible. However at the same time excessiveness and transgression of above instinct makes affairs of life difficult, sometimes may make it impossible, and similar is the case with other instincts. Among three types of patience mentioned earlier, patience against sin means offering resistance against the fire of rage or diversion of instinctive passions, because basically sin or transgression against God's law is nothing but acts of diversion, transgression, and aggression of instincts. Human beings are naturally inclined to endeavor for arranging necessities of life and other essential requirements. Since this could not be accomplished without having wealth and money, therefore motive to earn money and wealth constitutes a natural instinct.

Also, Islam being a school of mankind and way of life, encourages above instinct and certifies it by putting its own signature. Of course, it does so for right administration of society and accordingly establishes methods, procedures, and limitations, but never stops human beings from making endeavors for earning a genuine livelihood. In spite of all that, in many instances, this instinct of love for money and hoarding of wealth takes its roots in human soul like a chronic disease and with the result, money no longer remains as a means for providing requirement. Rather it turns into an intense desire for executing inhuman goals or tools of self-glorification, which is condemned from Islamic point of view. It's here that Islam decrees its followers to be patient through offering resistance against transgression, and diversion of instinctive forces. Other example of human instinct could be love for power since through their nature human beings crave for it.

Certainly those who have accepted weakness, and humility as essential elements of their existence must believe that they have deviated from assigned human nature. Islam, in this regards too, utilizes same approach as it does for dealing with all other instinctive desires. On one side efforts and endeavors in the path of achieving power have been commended as something desirable and permissible, and in certain circumstances even considered as compulsory. Yes! Islam considers power necessary where it's required for establishing truth, for discharging of important social obligations, reinstatement of lost rights of their rightful owners, and execution of divine commands and decrees. In these cases Islam has made it mandatory for all Muslims to gain power. While on the other hand, in Islam, path of this instinct towards aggression and ambitions has been closed. When instinct of love for power results in tyranny, oppression, brute force and savage crimes, this has been condemned as an undesirable and forbidden act. It's possible that association with a powerful tyrant or with a destructive organization may bring ample power for an ambitious person, but Islam never sanctions such an association, because act of associating with a tyrant is a direct support for strengthening tyranny. Balance of power which results from this kind of association is responsible for commitment of crimes. Here decrees of Islam and the Holy Qur'an are in direct confrontation with outburst and diversion of human instincts and closes path for them. Muslims are ordered to struggle and offer resistance against motives of this type of love for power, which results in mischief and corruption, and should never surrender to such ambitious tyrants—which means patience against sin. There are other examples of instincts such as sexual desires, love for fame, love for life, and etc, which could also be likewise examined, resulting in a better understanding of important individual and social issues.

6.5. Importance of Patience Against Sin

In the light of this brief discussion and in accordance with traditions and Islamic learning which are generally full of social education, it may be concluded that patience against sins and transgressions has been assigned a special importance. According to a few short traditions dealing with special circumstances, giving a constructive lesson for endeavoring Muslims of Impeccable Imams' (AS) period, this branch of patience has been considered a crucial support, and assigned a very special privilege. Perhaps it may be that because of offering patience in obedience there is something accompanied with natural desire or instinct existing within human beings, which is responsible for action and efforts. While on the other hand in order to resist desires for diversions, and not to surrender to appealing attractions of various obstacles—which are full of sweet and desirable natural attractions—is the field of patience against sin.

Therefore, practicing patience in obedience although means struggling against natural instinctive[1] attractions such as human desires for ease and comfort, nevertheless it's accompanied and supported by another natural instinct however weak. But patience against sin or transgression against God's laws, is in total and direct confrontation with all natural instinctive attractions and pleasures, and accordingly this kind of struggle is more difficult and therefore has been assigned a very special privilege. Also, patience against sins plays a determining role as far as the social affairs are concerned and since its effect is relatively more conspicuous, therefore this could be another reason for assigning a very special privilege to this kind of patience.

[1] This instinct is a part of real human structure, although its transgression and diversion is something unnatural and undesirable which should be resisted by human beings.

Chapter-7: Historical Examples

For example let us consider two very prominent faces of Islamic history and compare them with each other. One of them is enlightened, honorable, exciting while the other one is hated and condemned. These two faces belong to two persons who have been offered exactly similar and equivalent opportunities. Or it may be said that they both traveled together and reached simultaneously at an intersection, and in action each one selected a different direction. One of them because of choosing right path becomes the greatest and most honorable Islamic personality, and another one, because of his choosing wrong path becomes the most detested and deplorable face of the Islamic history. One of them is Omar bin Sa'd who is the Commander of Umayyad Army to suppress uprising of Imam al-Husain ibn Ali's (AS) uprising.

Other one is Hur bin Yazid Riyahi[1] who is another commander of same army, had been dispatched earlier on an assignment to follow and keep strict vigilance on Imam al-Husain's (AS) and his followers' movements, and had already committed an act of aggression against Imam al-Husain's (AS) revolutionary army. Each of them started their march on the road almost simultaneously. Ruling Umayyad regime was being threatened by a revolutionary force. Revolutionary freedom-giving fire was behind the ashes all over Hejaz and was about to ignite inside Iraq. Imam al-Husain ibn Ali (AS) considering Islamic obligations and realizing great responsibility upon his shoulders had taken a giant revolutionary step through uprising against Umayyad's corrupt and dictatorial regime. He took this giant heroic step to register forever in Islamic history the most practical and

---

1. Hur on the morning of Aashura came over to Imam Husain's (AS) camp and preferred to die as a martyr.

fundamental lesson for coming generations. This uprising therefore was a dangerous and a serious threat for ruling regime, and naturally it was forced to mobilize all resources at its disposal to suppress and crush this revolutionary uprising. Above two persons—Omar bin S'ad and Hur bin Yazid—were part of vast resources of that tyrant regime, which were mobilized against this revolutionary movement and against its founder Imam al-Husain ibn Ali (AS).

Therefore, in the very beginning both these persons manifested themselves as two important pawns of chess play on playground for game which was actually being played by an usurper caliph—Yazid ibn Mu'awiyeh. They were caliph's mercenaries to execute his decisions and commands in Karbala. But apart from that, they[1] too voluntarily accepted this assignment for the sake of their love for self, material gains, and desires and temptations aroused by their animal instincts. Omar bin S'ad came to Karbala because of his obsession for achieving power and position. Since his birth he was ignorant about religion and faith, for him promise made by Caliph for Governorship of the City of Ray—presently southern suburb of modern Tehran—was the most valuable and dearest thing than Yazid and obedience to his command. Hur bin Yazid too started his assignment for accomplishing similar goals. Both of them were aware that whatever they were going to accomplish meant committing a sin and a major one. But human passions and transgression of instinct for power and ambitions did not allow them to ponder about consequences of their would-be assignment—war with Imam al-Husain (AS), and ultimately put them on road which terminated into the most filthiest and beastly happening in human history.

Both of them were faced with most critical and sensitive decisions of their lives. One of road was leading them towards sensual desires which are same natural instincts such as love for power and ambitions, while the other one was leading them towards discharging their Islamic duty through joining righteous forces of Imam al-Husain (AS). At this critical juncture, thing which could

1. This has been explained by Fatima (SA) Imam Husain's (AS) daughter in her sermon in Kufa.

have rescued both of them was supposed to be—nothing else but patience. Yes! Through practicing patience one may overcome these destructive selfish passions. These strange destructive forces can only be controlled through the power of patience. Patience may enable you to resist against temptations for committing sins and transgression of God's Command. At this sensitive and determining moment, Omar bin S'ad could not resist against these deadly passions, and therefore terribly failed. The knotted rope of love for power and position was fallen over his neck, and he was being pulled towards hell. Although being a powerful and strong person, he was helpless to offer any resistance about his being fallen into this disgrace. Eventually he was overcome with impatience and was vanquished by motives of lust for power. And finally pulled through the rage of deadly instinctive passions, fell down all the way into the bottom of hell. Hur bin Yazid too encountered same situation, he too was being confronted with a critical dilemma. Had he allowed himself to be led by desires and passions of his soul, he too would have completed the assignment satisfactorily—which was assigned to him by Yazid—and would have ignored awakening inner voice of his conscience through believing himself to be only an executioner of orders issued by caliph, and thus could have achieved highest position of power.

For him if Governorship of the City of Ray was not into consideration, certainly something equivalent to that was kept in mind. For he too, after all was a human being, and therefore a knotted rope of greed, desire, and rage of instinctive passions was tied to his neck that was pulling him towards hell. He was pulled almost to the brink of fire i.e. line dividing two opposing camps in the plains of Karbala. Imam al-Husain's (AS) camp was manifestation of ready paradise, fountainhead of genuine Islamic values, splendor of human spirit, and defender of real Islam. It was in a direct face to face confrontation with Yazidi camp, which was manifestation of ready hell, degradation and humility of mankind, scene of hypocrisy, deceit and lies, and bastion of ignorance which, in the name of Islam was imposed upon Islamic society. Yes! Negative forces of degradation pulled him up to these limits i.e. brink of hell, but suddenly a heroic grand power, an awakening from within, at right moment took control of him and rescued him from this sudden fall. It gave him a severe jolt and sheared off the rope of desires and passions which was tied to his neck.

Through offering resistance against this violent instinctive passion, and through remaining patient against this great sin, which was tantamount to waging war against the forces representing total truth for the sake of forces which were complete manifestation of total blasphemy; not only did Hur rescue himself, but jumped into the kingdom of paradise from the very brink of fire. In above event there is a lesson for those who are interested in profound studies of human history. It clearly shows importance of this branch of patience against sin, in organizing great struggle between truth and falsehood, which ultimately determines the interpretation of history, and decides the destiny of a society.

7.1. Some other Examples of Patience against Sin

In order to study in detail examples of this branch of patience, we must recollect a series of different kind of deviations and great sins. It will be proved that patience has played most crucial role in each situation, such as follows:

A powerful strong mounted fist has been raised and is about to fall over the head of an innocent person, and there is absolutely no obstacle in its path—is a scene requiring this branch of patience. The strong instinctive forces consisting of anger, pride, selfishness, and other desires, urge this raised fist to strike against innocent person's head. In this situation patience means offering resistance against these instinctive motives and to control oneself against committing this transgression. Someone may have an easy access to lot of money and wealth, only if he could cross over the bridge, namely committing a murder, or indulging in a sinful act. Here natural lust for love of wealth, an extremely violent deviated instinctive force, takes control of the person to commit that crime. Here patience means offering resistance against these motives, and to ignore potential gains at the cost of a crime or sin. This may be regarded as another example of practicing this branch of patience. Sexual urges are extremely powerful and intense, which may be compared to a swamp, which swallows the elephants together with its drivers. It's exactly for the reason that this super magical characteristic had been exploited as an easy and suitable means for humiliating and degrading towering great human souls, by the enemies of human progress and exaltedness throughout the history. Patience in these situations means resisting powerful sexual urges, through not indulging into a lower shameful sexual act. Fear or danger are common characteristics which are common among ordinary people. It could be a product of many instincts or may consist of a single instinct.

However in many situations it plays a key role in bringing all kinds of humiliation, insults, imprisonment, crimes and catastrophes. In many instances weak individuals under influence of fear or danger submitted themselves to perform most lowly shameful tasks as well as committed horrible crimes, and ultimately lost their lives, wealth, position, honor, prestige, and children. In one instance they fell down from highest peaks of human exaltedness and lowered themselves to become simply a tool without any determination in the hands of enemies. Endurance against these forces of violence and corruption could be regarded as another scene for display of this branch of patience.

7.2. Review of Some Narrations

Here it would be worthwhile to ponder over some of narrations regarding this branch of patience, which have been narrated by Impeccable Imams (AS), and are full of important revealing lessons. Asbagh bin Nabatah who is a companion of Imam Ali (AS) quotes from him as follows:

"There are two types of patience, one of them is patience during tragedies or catastrophes, which is very good and charming, but there is another type of patience, which is far better and more charming than above, i.e. patience against God's forbidden acts."

—Al-Kafi, v.2.

Second Narration

Here Imam J'afar al-Sadiq (AS) quotes the Holy Prophet's (SAW), prediction of the state of affairs of his community as follows:

"The people will face a period in which power and authority will come only through bloodshed and brute oppression. Wealth will be amassed through usurping the rights of others and by stinginess. Love will be realized only through giving up faith and pursuing carnal desires. Whoever should find that period; should have patience in poverty because it will be better than faith; patience against grudge because it will be better than love; and patience against humility because it's better than honor. God will grant the reward of fifty truthful persons who believed in the Prophet."

—Al-Kafi, v.2.

This prediction was witnessed by Muslims of that time during shameful life of Mu'awiyeh, his son Yazid, and their successor caliphs, whereby wealth and other financial comforts could had been achieved only through means of usurpation of rights of deprived, transgression of weaker classes, exploitation of masses, stinginess and restrictions in financial dues, and indifference to genuine demands of deprived masses. Or in other words the Holy Prophet (SAW) predicted that natural development of Islamic community would not be such that each individual will be possessing plenty of wealth and material comforts without inflicting least injury to rest of the community—i.e rest of community would still have fair opportunities to earn wealth and other material comforts. Rather gaining wealth and other material comforts, through a certain special class could had been made possible only through transgressing and exploiting rights of rest of the community. This prediction was also witnessed as Islamic community transformed into various social classes.

Popularity or fame could had been only accomplished through discarding spirit of faith from one's life and existence, and completely submitting to carnal desires of self. In other words love of masses or corrupt leaders could had been achieved only through practicing flattery, lies, hypocrisy, cheating, surrendering to desires and passions, deceiving and making people feel proud, covering up blunders, not portraying realities and disregarding famous notion of encouraging good and discouraging forbidden acts *(amr bil maroof wa nahi anil munkar)*, etc. The Holy Prophet's (SAW) above prediction was full of wisdom, foretelling would-be state of affairs of the Islamic community in the near future in which level of thinking and insight of people will be lowered, Islamic values will decline, Islamic judicial system will be degraded, and general affairs of Muslims will become chaotic. It's of course obvious, that these happenings in the life of Islamic community, which was founded upon pillars of real Islamic values, or in other words the train of that community which started its journey on the rails of Islamic thoughts and ideology, was not possible without active involvement and subversive acts of some powerful, hidden, and mischievous hands operating to execute a calculated plan to destroy the Islamic community from within.

The Holy Prophet's (SAW) above prophecy clearly throws light about usurpation of political power, which may be regarded as most inhuman act in the Islamic history. Yes! The Holy Prophet (SAW) warned about these would-be occurrences. Alas! They happened too soon; when people appeared before the Commander of Faithful, Imam Ali (AS), they witnessed in his sayings and deeds, nothing but seriousness and decisiveness, for correcting deviated state of affairs of the Islamic community through pulling all violators and sinners before the court of law. And to obtain God's justice for their violations and transgressions, to restore lost genuine rights of rightful owners. His brother Aqeel when approached him to seek a financial favor, had to face a red hot iron bar and was turned down with a sad reply. Aqeel or any other person, when he approached Mu'awiyeh, was welcomed with smiling face, open arms, and rewarded with plenty of ready money.

It was therefore natural that persons whose conscience was not influenced by the logic of Islamic thoughts were more inclined towards Mu'awiyeh than Imam Ali (AS). Therefore, this consideration that Mu'awiyeh lacked fame and popularity during his rein is not correct. Notwithstanding the fact that people of Medina and Kufa, who were under direct influence of towering personality of Imam Ali (AS) and familiar with basics of Islamic ideology, rest of people of Islamic lands, throughout Mu'awiyeh's rein, because of suffocation of free thinking and enquiry, propaganda practiced through Umayyad bands, special characteristics of people for loving to be mercenaries of regime, considered Mu'awiyeh a competent, respectable, and charismatic personality. They even bestowed upon him honorable title of the Maternal Uncle of Muslims *(Khal al-Muslimeen)*,[1] i.e. the maternal uncle of believers. Of course, this fame and popularity was achieved by means of special tactical conduct of Mu'awiyeh with influential tribal chiefs who had considerable domination over masses, and some manipulated them to lower their heads before Mu'awiyeh. For these services they were showered with unlimited affection, blessed with plenty of wealth and power, and their hands were allowed openly to commit all kinds of horrible crimes and tortures against the poor deprived masses who possessed no other shelter.

These chiefs, in order to be benevolent towards their Lord of Bounties *(Vali-e-Nemat)*, and in order to maintain status quo, to exploit situation to their best advantage opened their tongues in praising him, and all of his faults and defects, or the type of faults he admired, were presented to masses as his exalted qualities and arts. This was the picture of would-be state of affairs of Islamic community as foreseen through prophetic eyes. Now in confronting with such a state of affairs and facing an incompetent and sinister regime, what were the obligations of people? The answer to this question was provided by the narration in previous pages.

---

[1] Since Mua'wiyeh's sister Umm-e-Habibeh was the Holy Prophet's (SAW) wife, and like his other spouses was called as Mother of Believers. With this misconstrued logic Mua'wiyeh's father Abu-Sufyan—a hard-core heathen would be called as the—Grandfather of Believers and his wife Hind, the eater of the Holy Prophet's (SAW) uncle Martyr Hamzeh's liver would be called as—the Grandmother of Believers!

Anyone who happens to face that period as predicted by the Holy Prophet (SAW) either in the near or distant future, must remain steadfast while facing poverty and indigence and should offer resistance against instinctual motives for hoarding wealth and possessing other material benefits. While he had option to act like his contemporaries, who through utilizing usual means, were busy in accumulation of wealth and other material gains, and passed through this difficulties naively, as though nothing unusual had happened. He too, through accepting filth, indulging in crimes, submitting to insults and captivation, giving up his dignity, honor, and exaltedness, and turning his back against all values and ideals, could have achieved comfortable and luxurious life and therefore would have fulfilled his carnal desires.

He should close his eyes over wealth, power and riches in his reach, at the cost of bringing poverty and destitution for thousands of people, as well as over hot and delicious food for him, at the cost of hunger for unlimited number of destitute masses. He should endure patiently for remaining lonely, unknown and blamed against instinctive motives of desiring status, fame and popularity. While having option of receiving favor of ignorant masses or leaders with vested interests, through opening his tongue for flattery, praise, lies, deceit and shutting up his lips for supporting truth, closing his eyes for encouragement of good and forbiddance of evil, and conscientiously electing to do otherwise.

Realizing divine obligations entrusted to him, and his personal duties, with full awareness he accepts demotion of his status, becomes hated in the eyes of tyrants, and lets his prestige and honor be usurped and trampled by oppressors. He should be patient and satisfied for possessing only lower social status and tolerate deprivation from higher prestigious positions offering better material gains and power. He should not opt for accepting titles and important positions of power at the cost of committing inhuman shameful crimes. God's reward for someone who practices above advices in his deeds, would be equivalent to the reward earned by fifty righteous believers during the Holy Prophet's (SAW) period. Therefore, this heavenly saying which emanates from a celestial heart and whose value is tantamount to a divine revelation, while offering the most important and in-depth training regarding social issues, also reflects meanings and value of this branch of patience—against sin.

7.3. Patience Against Unpleasant Events—Tragedies

Human life is always accompanied by events and unpleasant calamities, and there is no escape from such happenings. Human structure has been created in such a way, that it has to deal with these imposed situations, i.e. always encountering unpleasant events and calamities during entire span of our lives. The following famous sentence of the Commander of Faithful, Imam Ali (AS) describes the above theme as follows:

"The world is like a house which has been encircled with temptations and calamities."

Sickness, physical handicaps, financial losses, death of loved ones, and deprivations are some of few examples of inevitable happenings from which there is no escape. Even the most prosperous class of people are not immune against these types of occurrences. When such calamities befall naturally without any choice or intention of our own, in our lives, usually there are two types of reactions shown by the people, as follows:

1. Some people on account of calamity give up their resistance completely and therefore become spiritually handicapped.

2. Other group of people, bear with patience considering it a natural thing of this worldly life, and come out of it intact with dignity.

According to famous Persian poet Roudaki[1] the merit, greatness, and leadership of a man is tested during his encounter with calamity. Grief, crying, and lamentation which are the ways of

---

[1]. J'afar bin Mohammad Roudaki regarded as the father of Persian Poetry, flourished in the Samanid Court at Bukhara in the 9-10th century AD. [Tr]

weak, timid-hearted and impatient individuals, in itself is a strong natural passion. Which imposes a violent emotional force upon human structure, whereby all body parts are employed to perform a particular function. Eyes shed tears, tongue complains, throat groans, hands, feet, and head, are all involved in performing special actions and movements. Patience, against calamities means not to surrender to these violent emotional outbursts. A patient human being, while facing such tragedies does not give up his morale and maintains his composure and control. These tragedies do not make him depressed and discouraged, and do not stop him from making efforts and endeavors for accomplishing main goals in real life. Therefore, this type of patience against calamities is also important, and has been termed as fair and charming in the narration quoted earlier. Now, let us consider the case of a wayfarer who starts his journey in a certain direction so that he could reach the final desired destination. If upon encountering each unpleasant accident, and after receiving a small injury, he gives up his morale and looses his composure, then it's obvious that such a person will never complete this journey and reach final destination. Resistance, offered against these motives of depression, while facing these tragedies is a key factor, which not only secures high morale, but moreover, this endurance in itself, is an exercise, which is beneficial for building up determination and strong iron-will among human beings, which are pre-requisites for continuation of difficult journey. Therefore, patience against natural tragedies which befall upon human beings, without any option or choice, consists of following two important advantages:

Firstly, it secures and maintains high morale, which is responsible for all constructive involvement, and further acts as an obstacle to prevent it from getting lost or being destroyed completely.

Secondly, it builds up human determination or will power, which is an important means for all positive actions, and further it provides required endurance to face optional tragedies. Special encouragement and excitement shown by religious guardians about this type of patience, clearly demonstrates its constructive and miraculous role. In the following two narrations deep philosophy of this branch of patience could be clearly demonstrated.

First Narration

"Whoever has not equipped himself with the weapon of patience, during hardships and calamities of time, will be subjected to a state of weakness and helplessness."

—Al-Kafi, v.2, p-93.

Second Narration

"For a believer, if a position and rank, has been taken into consideration by God, which could never be accomplished by deeds alone; he is inflicted with physical sickness, or loss of wealth, or tragedies to his loved ones; and in case he remains patient, is awarded by God the assigned position and rank."

—Safinatul Bihar v.2, p-5

In the above narration constructive and exalted role of patience has been demonstrated explicitly. Othman bin M'azoon, who was an experienced Muslim and had migrated to Ethiopia and Medina, during early period of Islam, lost his young son in Medina. This tragedy was so devastative that he decided to spend all his remaining life inside his house in prayers, and suddenly stopped all his social involvement completely. His depression after the death of his young son was so intense, that he wished never to face the pleasures of life again. The Holy Prophet (SAW) after hearing about his state of affairs, paid him a courtesy visit and advised him to change his decision. The Holy Prophet (SAW) said that Islam does not allow monastic life of renunciation of world, sitting in an isolated corner, engaged in prayers only. Renunciation of world by Islamic community means, participation in struggle for the sake of God. Therefore, patience against unforeseen tragedies, for which we have no choice, means to be able to tolerate the injury caused by calamity without giving up morale, and to be able to continue routine normal involvement of real life, and eventually forgetting tragedy with the passage of time.

7.4. Patience Against Optional Tragedies

This branch of patience surpasses in excellence over other situations because in this case a conscientious, and aware human being arises to accomplish a certain goal, and offers resistance against all hardships and unpleasant events which are inflicted upon him during this course. But in spite of facing all these severe calamities he does not get demoralized, depressed, and continues his movement towards the cherished goal. If we perform an in-depth analysis for research purposes, regarding the state of affairs of human societies in history, looking for lofty human ideals, and specially goals aspired by divine prophets, which were always in conflict with the classes representing tyrants and profiteers, and therefore were always opposed by them.

It would become crystal clear that there had always been permanent war and confrontation between the proclaimers of these higher goals and powerful classes of tyrants and oppressors. There are plenty of verses in the Holy Qur'an which throw considerable light regarding historical confrontation between divine prophets and representative of false deities *(taghout)*. Since this confrontation between truth and falsehood is inevitable, therefore it's necessary for the followers of path of truth, proclaimers of justice and righteousness, and truth seekers and researchers following the path of divine prophets, to know and predict in advance that the path of truth is always accompanied by all kinds of hardships and calamities. The Holy Qur'an, in order to make believers ready for confronting problems, announces in advance clearly potential dangers on the path of truth and brings historical realities to their attention as follows:

"Assuredly you will be tried in your property and in your persons, and ye will hear much wrong from those who were given the scripture before you, and from the idolaters. But if ye preserve and ward off (evil), then that is of the steadfast heart of things."

—The Holy Qur'an (3: 186).

In reality those who wanted to live like a believer or God's slave, also wanted to be responsible towards divine obligations and other commitments assigned to them, realized that they will be opposed and subjected to different kind of hardships by their opponents, and they soon witnessed the truth of this Holy Qur'an's prediction with their own eyes in their own period. Of course, one who enjoys an important position, rank, and whose faith and actions are more determined in God's path would be more effective. Therefore, in the same proportion will be subjected to severe hardships and tragedies by opponents, whose tolerance is indeed difficult. There is a famous narration quoted from Imam J'afar al-Sadiq (AS): ***"Among all people, divine prophets were inflicted with harshest calamities, and after those who were closer to them subjected to similar kinds of hardships and calamities."***

—Safinatul Bihar

Of course, these calamities are not like type of unforeseen natural tragedies, as described earlier, for which a human being has absolutely no control or choice, rather in this case everyone has option to choose. In case, he desires and prefers comfortable and easy life of this world, and to remain immune against these types of calamities, he may elect to do so. What makes these events inevitable is movement towards the cherished goal. Every easy going person who prefers comfortable environment of his home and never takes trouble to venture outside the four walls of his house, would never face inconveniencies and problems encountered in a journey. But at the same time, he will never benefit from experiences which are possible only through going an adventurous journey. He would remain safe throughout his life from such events as, slipping from mountain peak, facing a beast in jungle, and being robbed by bandits, which are likely events of an adventurous journey. Like every naive and irresponsible human being who has not recognized aims of life, taken any steps towards that goal, and prefers an uneventful life without headaches, would be better advised to follow the decree of following verse of S'adi, the famous Iranian poet as follows:

"Beh darya der, manfeh bishomar ast,

Wa gar khahi salamat der kinar ast!"

English Translation:

"Although inside the sea there are plenty of material gains,

But if you prefer safety, better stay on the shore!"

According to this logic[1] one could easily choose the option to remain immune from all troubles, headaches, and injuries etc, which are a pre-requisite for joining the path of divine prophets. Therefore, calamities on the path of divine prophets are optional tragedies, in the sense that they are inflicted upon those, who are taking commands from the following saying of the Commander of Faithful, Imam Ali (AS): ***"Through taking giant steps on the divine path, they throw themselves into the whirlpool of tragedies."***

Therefore, they succeeded in announcing positive and definite reply to divine invitation to support the truth. Hence, patience against optional tragedies is important type of patience relative to other categories. This branch of patience reflects highest degree of human exaltedness in facing the optional tragedies. This type of patience means accepting tragedies in spite of the fact that all instinctual motives, are forcing him to turn his back in the middle of path and stop offering resistance any more; yet he continues offering resistance, and never feels sorry or ashamed to be inflicted with severe blows on the righteous path. Khabbab bin al-Arth, is ranked among top Muslims, who accepted the invitation of the Holy Prophet (SAW) to Islam, and offered a lot of sacrifices. Because of his conversion to Islam, he lost a significant portion of his property and possessions. One day, he complained to the Holy Prophet (SAW) about his severe financial loss. He himself narrates: ***"The Holy Prophet (SAW) had spread his robe on the ground, and was reclining with his back against the Holy K'aba. When he listened to my complaint, he changed his relaxed sitting position, and his composure changed,***

---

1. Like the French poet Gautier who once during wartime stated: ***"I prefer lying down to sitting, sitting to standing, and remaining home to going out. I will know nothing of war they say has engulfed the entire world, unless a bullet shatters the window of my house."*** [Tr]

and said: 'Your predecessors*[1] *sometimes were slaughtered by iron saw, cutting their skin, veins, and flesh all the way down till the bones. But they remained committed to their faith, and never complained, even when in some cases, their bodies were cut off into two equal pieces. God will carry this movement (Islam) till its perfection. The distance a rider travels between Sana*[2] *and Hadhramut*[3] *roads and highways will be so safe, under the Islamic state and system that nobody will be afraid of anything but God, and flock of sheep will not be scared of anyone but wolf. '"

Therefore, the Holy Prophet (SAW) through delivering these fiery speeches instilled his followers with the spirit of resistance and iron will, and encouraged them to be patient, while facing calamities which were inflicted upon them for the sake of their belief in God. It's quite possible that some one by practicing patience for discharging Islamic obligations i.e. patience in obedience, or by offering resistance against instinctual passions i.e. patience against sin, may be genuinely included in the list of believers and may start walking on the path whose other end leads to God. But once confronted with accidents and tragedies, which are essential and inevitable part of this journey, he may not withstand, and in the middle of path, face moral break down, weakness of faith, hopelessness, and other such reasons on account of impatience; decide to return without completing journey, disregarding discharge of his duties, which were assigned to him. Therefore, completion of journey on this path with certainty, and without any doubt for not breaking in the middle, is made possible only through practicing this type of patience i.e. patience against optional tragedies.

---

[1] The Holy Prophet (SAW) was referring to believers in the mission of earlier divine prophets, who in those distant times were subjected to all sorts of inhuman atrocities by idolaters. The main theme of messages of all divine prophets was Monotheism—belief in one and only God and Islam which means submission to God's will.

[2] Capital of Yemen.

[3] Region in the southern part of Yemen.

7.5. Ways for Encouraging this Branch of Patience

In view of its importance and fundamental role, many verses of the Holy Qur'an focus on this particular branch of patience, so that Muslims could feel the charm of this special struggle in their heart and spirit. One of the ways for being patient against optional tragedies is to ponder upon them which are beyond our control. In order that confrontation with death may not be difficult for wayfarers on God's path, the Holy Qur'an reminds us that: Death is destined for all human beings. Those who do not die on the battlefield will eventually die on their beds in their homes. Life and death all belong to God, and deeds which are accounted for His path carry the best of compensation and bonus from God.

"Muhammad is not but a messenger, messengers (the like of whom) have passed away before him. Will it be that, when he dieth or is slain, you will turn back on your heels? He who turneth back doth not hurt to God, and God will reward the thankful."

—The Holy Qur'an (3:144).

"O you who believe! Be not as those who disbelieved and said of their brethren who went abroad in the land or were fighting in field: If they had been (here) with us they would not have died or been killed; that God may make it anguish in their hearts. God giveth life and causeth death; and God is seer what ye do."

—The Holy Qur'an (3:156).

"Those who, while they sat at home, said of their brethren (who were fighting for the cause of God): If they had been guided by us they would not have been slain. Say (unto them, 0 Muhammad): Then avert death from yourself if ye are truthful."

—The Holy Qur'an (3: 168).

The other method consists of reminding progress accomplished by accepting these calamities on the desired path, and severe blows dealt to obstacles on the path by these means.

"Faint not nor grieve, for ye will overcome them if ye are (indeed) believers."

—The Holy Qur'an (3:139).

"If you have received a blow, the (disbelieving) people have received a blow the like thereof. These are (only) the vicissitudes which We cause to follow one another for mankind, to the end that God may know those who believe and may choose witnesses from among you, and God loveth not wrong-doers."

—The Holy Qur'an (3: 140).

The Holy Qur'an emphasizes upon its followers not to worry or be slow because victory eventually belongs to believers. If believers have received blows, similar blows were also dealt to the enemy. Third method consists of narratives of predecessors and their role against optional tragedies. The Holy Qur'an, puts the patience and steadfastness of supporters of divine prophets and pioneers of Islam in the following language:

"And with how many a prophet have there been a number of devoted men who fought (beside him). They quailed not for aught that befell them in the way of God, nor did they weaken, nor were they brought low. God loveth the steadfast."

—The Holy Qur'an (3: 146).

There are many such verses in the Holy Qur'an describing similar situations, and encouraging believers to tread the path of divine prophets. Of course, patience against such optional tragedies, while it's quite difficult and requires strong determination and faith, but at the same time, in itself plays a miraculous role in producing firm resolve and righteous faith; and more important than that is responsible for creation of ideal Islamic society. It's for this reason that the Holy Qur'an's many verses, and Impeccable Imams' (AS), authentic narrations emphasize in different styles the importance of this branch of patience, and have issued necessary guidelines and instructions about its practice. Since this discussion which is mostly based upon authentic narrations, therefore let us quote one more narration about the patience against all kinds of tragedies as follows:

"Abi Basir quotes from Imam J'afar Sadiq (AS): 'A free person is free in all situations, if a terrible tragedy befalls upon him he is patient, and tragedies and inflictions cannot break him. He might be arrested, chained and tyrannized but converts hardships into comfort like Prophet Joseph (AS) the righteous, whose freedom was least affected by oppression, tyranny, and imprisonment.'"

—Al-Kafi v.2, p-89.

Chapter-8: Advantages and Effects of Patience

In the end, it would be necessary to mention about the advantages and constructive effects of patience. Although in our earlier discussions, the topic has been covered to a certain extent, but in order to provide more detailed information regarding individual and social effects of patience, further discussion is necessary. It should be mentioned that, here we are not looking into advantages of patience in the next world, i.e. rewards which will be awarded in the hereafter to a person for being patient in this life. But at the same time, it should not be forgotten that those rewards cannot be separated with some advantages of patience in the life of this world. At present, however, we are looking into rewards and advantages of patience for a patient person, or a society and groups of patients, as a ready cash, on account of their being steadfast and patient, right here at this stage of worldly life.

It's really difficult to start and to select a certain advantage out of unlimited advantages of patience. One could say in nutshell that every thing in this world and next world, all higher noble human ideals, lowest mischievous plots, and in summary, each goal or aim desired by anyone are all directly tied to their being steadfast and patient. If it's required to produce a logical reasoning to support above statement, and if vast experiences gained by mankind throughout history are not sufficient enough for convincing, then let us present this definite and explicit formula: Accomplishment of a goal requires action, and action requires patience and endurance. Everyone must have at least a couple of times in his lifespan must have examined correctness of the above formula.

8.1. Permanence and Victory

The Commander of Faithful, Imam Ali (AS) in the following quotation, which is full of wisdom has said:

"A steadfast patient person would never be denied success, however it may materialize after a long time."

—Nahj al-Balagheh

In another quotation from him, the same theme has been described in other words as follows:

"Whoever mounts the horse of patience would definitely find his path to the field of victory."

—Nahj al-Balagheh

During the Battle of Siffin, in an inspiring sermon for boosting the morale of his forces, the Commander of Faithful, Imam Ali (A.S.) said:

"Make your supports upon righteousness and patience because it's only after patience that victory shall be bestowed upon you."

—Tarikh Kamil ibn Athir.

Is it really true, that patience and endurance will enable a person to achieve his goal? If this is a overall law or regulation, which is always applicable, then why all along the history, we encounter many groups, who in spite of their best efforts, endurance, and steadfastness could not accomplish their desired goals, and could not witness the victory. During the early period of Islam, there are incidents like A'ashura, uprisings of Tawwabin[1] and Zaid bin Ali (AS)[2] and similar incidents during later periods.

Of course many people are interested to know the answer to above questions, but if we ponder a little bit, it will become explicitly clear. In our opinion, those who consider these historical incidents apparently unsuccessful and inconclusive events, such as A'ashura, and Zaid bin Ali's (AS) martyrdom, as a violation of overall law—after patience comes victory—have not recognized the aims and objects, which were incorporated in each of these incidents, and whose attainment meant achieving success and victory for these movements. Now let us ask this question. What were the aims of these historical events? If this question could be answered correctly, it would become quite apparent that under no circumstances they were defeated or disappointed in their endeavors and efforts toward achieving their cherished goals and objectives.

Incidentally, it should be reminded, that aims and objectives, as regards to being long term or short term, differ from each other. Some of aims could be accomplished in short time, while some others could only be materialized after a prolonged period. To plant a sapling, to nurture it, and make all other necessary arrangements, are preliminary

---

1. Tawwabin or penitents, as they are called in history books, were mostly people of Kufa and Iraq, who rose up against Umayyad rule in 64 AH, three years after the tragedy of Karbala to avenge the blood of Imam Husain (AS) and the Holy Prophet's (SAW) Household. Led by the Prophet's ageing companion Suleiman ibn Surad al-Khazaei, who was one of the leading Islamic generals in the conquest of Transoxiana, their sole aim in battle, was either to kill the ungodly Umayyad or to achieve martyrdom in the process. For almost two years, they fought the caliph's forces, killing a great number of those troops who had fought against Imam al-Husain (AS) at Karbala. [Tr]

2. Zaid bin Ali (AS) was the fourth Imam Ali ibn al-Husain's (AS) son—the survivor of Karbala. Fed up with the Umayyad tyranny, he started an uprising in Iraq and was tragically martyred and his body was burned by caliph's forces in 124 AH. His movement like other Alawite uprisings, aroused people's conscience against the libertine and ungodly rule of Umayyad, who were swept into the dustbin of history ten years later in 132 AH. [Tr]

requirements, in order to utilize fruits of that tree. If all these preliminary requirements were, without least negligence, fulfilled timely, and if precautions were taken to make it resist negative factors responsible for unproductiveness and decay—certainly this plant will bear fruits, but a uniform and fixed period for all the places does not exist.

Sometimes fruits under consideration will be obtained, say after a period of one year. But occasionally depending upon the type of tree, fruits under consideration, and natural circumstances are such that one cannot hope to have them at least before ten years. Certainly, ultimate goal for taking care of this sapling, which will be achieved after ten years, is to have desired fruits of this tree. But during all these long waiting years, the aim behind each year's efforts is to move sapling one step closer to the date when it will bear fruits. After passing of each progressive year, gardener becomes happy and satisfied, that his efforts during past years have produced results i.e. sapling has grown through one stage, getting on a year closer to its fruit-bearing date.

Now, if an observer, aware of efforts and endeavors of this hardworking and patient gardener all along the year; does not see any fruits on the tree after passing of a year, and wrings his hands in hopelessness; looses his confidence in the famous notion: ***It's only after patience, victory would have a chance;*** out of immaturity and inexperience were to criticize the gardener. Then such an observer would obviously be termed a narrow minded and impatient person by every one and would be reminded that he should not expect that efforts and endeavors of one year will produce a result equivalent to ten years of efforts.

The movement of A'ashura, and all other later movements having same orientation and same direction, without exception succeeded in achieving their desired aims and goals. Each of these movements were giant strides for destruction of power of tyrants ruling in the name of Islam, and for establishment of an ideal Islamic society. Without any doubt following these pioneering giant steps, if courage of later generations would have encouraged them, to take next steps—the ultimate result would have been certainly achieved. Therefore, to expect that ultimate result, which could only be obtained through organized and continuous efforts and involvement of a few generations, or few persons, or some people of a single generation—is certainly wrong resulting from ignorance and over expectation.

In the above example, it should be said to the impatient and inexperienced observer; that those who had accepted hardships of gardening and discharged their duties understood well that the work done by them, each day and each hour, had instantaneously produced desired results, even before passing of that hour and day; and they achieved the result of their patience practiced at each passing instant. Two years of hard work of this gardener brings fruit-bearing date closer to two years. If his efforts were not there, fruits of this sapling would have been delayed by two years or perhaps two years of fruit-bearing time would have been wasted. Is reality other than this? Parallel to this reality, there exists another reality too. If, after an obstacle which prevented the sincere gardener from continuing his job, another gardener does not pursue the duties of his predecessor, by undertaking the planned activities for the third, and fourth years—obviously this tree will never bear fruits.

Let us consider the example of a certain load, supposed to be carried to a place, say ten steps ahead. Now, suppose it has moved by two steps, one could say the load has reached close to its final destination by two steps. If the first person, responsible for its delivery, is in a position to undertake the remaining steps, he would do so, if not his substitute will take the remaining steps to carry the load to its final destination. But if this responsibility, i.e. moving the load past remaining eight steps was not discharged by first person or by his substitute, then obviously load will never be delivered to its final destination. However, there is no doubt, that the result of patience in taking first two pioneering steps has been achieved—because load has moved by two steps.

To uproot a deep rooted tree, and to remove a huge rock without having proper equipment like drill, chain saw, or powerful and strong hands, is of course not possible, but having all of them, but not having patience will not produce any result. If first person having strong hands and patience, after making a headway was forced to discontinue his efforts, then others who were supposed to take his place, are responsible to carry on the job by one more step ahead, and another stage closer to success. Likewise, Zaid bin Ali's (AS), uprising because of an unexpected tragedy—an arrow struck him on his forehead and he fell down instantly—could not accomplish the final victory, but the result of this pioneering step i.e. to arise was achieved immediately by him. His uprising was a heavy blow to the huge rock of usurper Umayyad regime. A heavy rock, which required repeated and continuous blows, to be destroyed completely. If initial blows would have been accompanied by later blows, this black boulder of Umayyad rule, which was a heavy burden upon the Islamic community, and a source of oppression, would have splintered into pieces. Certainly, without initial severe blow being struck, later blows would not have achieved that desired result, or may be, no one would have dared to struck those later blows. There are narrations which consider the Lord of Martyrs, Imam al-Husain's (AS) martyrdom as the key factor for collapse of Sufyanid rule and Zaid bin Ali's (AS) martyrdom for Marwanid's[1] downfall.

8.2. Psychological Traces of Patience in Individuals' Lives

Apart from constructive social advantages of patience such as gaining victory and fulfillment of aims and goals, this characteristic is also responsible for positive and very important influences upon the mentality and spirit of patient person. It's because of this miraculous awareness that most of historical human sacrifices, and specially epic and supreme sacrifices of Karbala's martyrs, i.e. the companions and relatives of the Lord of Martyrs—Imam al-Husain (AS), whose memories we are celebrating during these nights[2] will become easy

---

1. The Umayyad who usurped power of Islamic State in 41 AH, when Mu'awiyeh bin Abu Sufyan, forced Imam al-Hasan (AS) to abdicate, were divided into two branches; the Sufyanid whose rule terminated with Mu'awiyeh ibn Yazid's death in 64 AH. (683 AD) and Marwanids, whose rule started with Marwan ibn Hakam and ended with Marwan ibn Muhammad al-Hemar in 132 AH, when a new dynasty Abbasid usurped the power. [Tr]

2. These speeches were delivered during Muharram of 1394 AH at the Masjid-e-Karamat in Mashad, Khorasan, I.R. Iran. [Tr]

to comprehend. What we mean with spiritual mentality they are influences left by patient person upon his soul and mind that even before accomplishing external and definite results of his struggle—he instantaneously obtains the personal result.

8.3. Birth of Invincible Spirit

Foremost positive and constructive effect of patience is to produce a strong and invincible personality. Like a good physical exercise program makes a person strong and healthy to enable him to offer better physical resistance. Secondly, it produces all required elements for achieving success in accomplishment of aims, fulfillment of desires, be material or ideological, among patient individuals. Defeats and failures suffered during social, religious, and ideological struggle would have a devastative moral effect, a blow, inflicted by vincible and week mentality upon one's determination to carry on struggle, whose damage and devastation is many times severe than losses inflicted by trained professional armed forces and their armament. The soldier[1] who decided to run away from battlefield turning his back to enemy has indeed first suffered a moral defeat—before giving up his physical strength. Until this psychological defeat is not inflicted upon him, it's impossible that a soldier will be able to turn his back and run away from the battlefield.

The historic behavior of Tariq bin Ziyad, the brave Commander of Muslim Army—the victor of a portion of Spain in the year 94 AH, 711 AD, who after crossing the Mediterranean Sea and stepping upon the enemy land, ordered burning of all his ships, is an example of this invincible spirit. The prime quality of patience is to produce such an invincible spirit in a patient person. Those individuals, who while facing routine events of day-to-day life, such as financial losses, sickness, frustration, hatred, and death etc do not offer resistance and endurance, very soon become dejected, aggrieved, annoyed, and

---

[1] General George C. Marshall, a great soldier had stated that you can have all material in the world, but without morale it's largely ineffective. He also said: It's not enough to fight, rather the spirit which we bring to fight decides ultimate outcome. It's morale that wins the victory. [Tr]

helpless when confronted with obstacles in their path, and therefore ran away from the scene of struggle and were susceptible to an instant defeat.

Contrary to these individuals of weak mentality there are those, who in confronting every event in their life use patience as their ultimate winning weapon, and offer resistance in the best possible manner, achieving an invincible morale and strong will power to face the problems of life. An impatient person could be compared to a soldier in the battlefield who is fighting virtually naked without amour. Such an ill-equipped soldier is most likely to be killed and disappear from the scene during very first encounter. With the same analogy a patient person could be compared to a soldier who is clad in a coat of mail from head to toes, and is fully equipped with all required armaments. Obviously to defeat such a well equipped soldier by the enemy would be a relatively a difficult task.

The one, who would never be defeated in the battlefield of life, who had already made all necessary arrangements, through putting on amour of patience. Such a person, never gets defeated easily, and when faced with problems and unpleasant events, which are abound at every step on the road of perfection and prosperity, never flinches his eyebrows, and his legs and heart remain firm and stable without showing least signs of trembling. The following narration from Imam al-Sadiq (AS) throws ample light about the depth of this divinely inspired Islamic characteristic:

"Anyone who has not prepared for himself the logistics of patience to meet every tragedy will find himself in a state of despair and helplessness."

—Tohf al-Aqool.

It means that one who has not planned in advance, and developed within himself a spirit of resistance would soon find himself in a state of despair and helplessness while encountering problems and unexpected tragedies in his life. Exactly opposite to this, if one has equipped himself with logistics of patience for confrontation with tragedies shall never face disappointment and defeat. The secret of steadfastness and permanence of great builders of history of mankind, and foremost amongst them, the divine prophets and other pious statesmen, who in spite of being inflicted with most severe pains and tortures at the very beginning of their invitation, remained relatively active and stable, lies in the same point. With an accurate foresight regarding bitterness and unpleasantness of this path, and with their properly being equipped with logistics of patience, they were able to completely eliminate possibilities of their psychological defeat and with the result converted themselves into robust and invincible creatures. Their opponents and enemies that in many instances were equipped with all kinds of resources became tired and helpless, but these great men in spite of being deprived of proper resources diligently continued their heroic invincible resistance. Mutawakkil the Abbasid[1] caliph once said: ***"Ibn al-Rida[2] has put me in a state of bewilderment."***

How someone like Imam Hadi (AS),[3] who has spent most of period of his leadership under intense pressure of ruling regime of caliph Mutawakkil, was in a position to put the powerful caliph in a state of annoyance. When one among the two combatant adversaries is weak as regards to outwardly resources, but in spite of being faced with imprisonment, deprivations, away from comfortable and secured environment does not get harassed; pressures and hardships do not break his iron will, and in spite of all these obstacles on

---

1. Mutawakkil: One of Abbasid caliphs who was specially hostile to Ahl al-Bayt (AS) and their followers ruled from 232 AH/847 AD to 247 AH/861 AD. [Tr]

2. After Imam al-Rida (AS) eighth Imam, three successive imams till eleventh imam and some other prominent descendants of eighth imam, during that period were called Ibn al-Rida (AS). In the above sentence reference is to Imam Hadi (AS) the tenth imam.

3. Important point in this narration is importance of predicting dangers in advance, while making preparations for struggle. Perhaps, those who without considering potential dangers, conducted a dangerous operation, do not have strength to confront the danger and therefore as soon as they faced the signs of potential danger, became disappointed, ashamed, and helpless.

the path of his cherished goals, continues his long term march. It's obvious that his adversary who, in spite of having equipped with better material resources lacks commitment and strong spiritual faith, and therefore becomes easily harassed and defeated. This is the strange characteristic of patience which makes a person invincible.

8.4. Appearance of Righteous Virtues Within

People before testing, cannot evaluate themselves, and very often are unaware about hidden energy in their existence. Let us consider the example of a strong person, who is possessed with plenty of natural physical strength without doing any special practice or physical exercise. Let us imagine that he has never participated in a weight lifting or any other physical competition, such a person is certainly not aware regarding the amount of physical strength in his body. We could only discover God given energy in our existence, when we are challenged to participate in a certain competition which requires utilization of that particular energy. The second important effect of patience is, that a patient person after offering resistance in different fields of life and against events and obstacles, discovers about the amount of energy, its particulars, and noble and higher sublime virtues hidden within his existence, which were never discovered by him earlier, during a routine life without any headache.

Those who have suffered pressures and harshness of life, and for the sake of their cherished noble aims and ideals, were subjected to severe tragedies and hardships appreciate above meanings. Such individuals with an irreversible decree of determination, in their confrontation with great dangers, and severe pressures—while a strange naive observer would have considered them defeated and destroyed completely—because of their patience and endurance, were able to achieve a sense of relief and victory; an unprecedented power and surprising grandeur within their existence, which was something completely new for them and was never realized by them before. Therefore, it's because of patience, that a patient person could better recognize his self, as well as could better identify positive points within his existence, and could discover energy which was never identified throughout his life before.

8.5. More Attention and Reliance upon God

The third constructive quality of patience is that at whatever stage or extent a patient person may be, it helps him to bring relatively closer and more reliant upon God. Now, some people may consider that reliance upon God does not get along with reliance upon self, and therefore according to their logic, anyone who is dependent upon God, could not rely upon his self. When it's said: Rely upon God, such people complain and say: Let people rely upon themselves, and their eyes and hopes look towards themselves, as if one who invites people to rely upon God, wants them not to be relied upon themselves. While in reality for a person committed to God, reliance upon self is complimentary and inseparable with each other, even to the extent that reliance upon self is regarded as one of the parameter of patience, which in effect is a means for reliance upon God as well as. Because impatience against bitter tragedies of life, and fear against optional calamities, which are reflections of lack of self reliance, also means forgetting of God.

When a person is inflicted with severe tragedies of life, and millstone representing the testing of life is grinding him with intense pressure, if he does not become, impatient, aggrieved, and annoyed, channels of his communication with God would become wider and independent, and his heart and soul would be enlightened with God's illumination. And on the contrary, his becoming weak and annoyed, makes him ignorant, stranger and disconnected from his own self as well as from God. This sentence speaks about a reality fully explicit with clear reasoning and tested with experience of those, who in their confrontation with adverse conditions, were able to utilize patience as their winning weapon, and believe and acknowledge this matter with certainty.

"Our Lord! Bestow on us endurance, make our foothold sure, and give us help against the disbelieving folk."

—The Holy Qur'an (2:250).

Part-2: Prayer

"And as for those, who hold fast by the book and establish prayer, surely we never let the reward of righteous be perished."

—The Holy Qur'an (7: 170).

Persian Couplets:

Guft paighambar, rukoo ast wa sujood,

Bar dare haq kooftan halqeh wajood,

Halqehee aan dar, har aan koo mizanad,

Bahre ou doulat, sari berron kunad.

English Translation:

"The Holy Prophet (SAW) said that Rukoo and Sojood mean,

Knocking at God's Threshold the chain of yours existence.

Whoever knocks the chain of that door,

The esoteric wealth and salvation comes out for him."

—Molana[1]

---

[1]. Molavi: Molana Jalaluddin Muhammad (604-672 AH), son of Muhammad bin Khatibi famous as Baha-ud-din was the most famous scholar and mystic poet of Iran. Also his father was a great scholar and mystic of his time. He received his early education under the tutorship of his learned father, and later on after his father's demise, continued his studies under the famous scholar Burhanuddin Mohaqeq Tirmizi. The later encouraged him to pursue his higher studies at the prestigious literary learning center in Damascus. Molana met with Shams Tabrizi in 642 AH. This meeting has a tremendous impact upon him, and brought a great spiritual revolution in his personality. His most famous mystical poetry works are:

1- Mathnavi: Consists of six volumes, containing 26000 verses of poetry, describing the religious and Gnostic sublime realities in a simple language.

2. Divan-e-Kabir: Consisting of 50,000 mystical verses is another literary mystical masterpiece left by Molana. [Tr]

9. Translator's Forward—Prayer

The present book is compilation of speeches of Grand Ayatollah Sayyid Ali Khamenei—Supreme Leader of the Islamic Republic of Iran—that he delivered during Muharram of 1394 Hijri 1973 AD at the Masjid-e-Karamat, Mashad, Khorasan, I.R. Iran. These speeches contain extremely valuable information about the importance of prayer in our lives in accordance with verses of the Holy Qur'an and the Holy Prophet's (SAW) and Ahl al-Bayt's (AS) authentic traditions. Prayer has been described as the central pole *(amood)* which supports the entire tent of religion. If that pole isn't standing vertically the entire tent would collapse; prayer plays such a significant role in the religion. If prayer is accepted—all other deeds of a believer would also be accepted by God, however in case if prayer isn't accepted—then nothing would be accepted and one would face the Day of Sorrow (*Youm al-Hasrat)* with his fingers biting with teeth in vain.

Prayer in Islam could be divided into four basic forms namely: Ritual prayer *(salat)*, supplication *(dua)*, litany *(wird)* and invocation *(dhikr).* The first one in its mandatory form might be slightly compared to what is implied in Christianity as mass or holy communion—although this type of prayer in Islam is quite unique and can't be compared to any thing else. The second phrase supplication is equivalent to a personal prayer or simply prayer as the Christians generally used the term. The mandatory ritual prayer must be performed personally or in communion five times[1] a day

[1] The Holy Prophet (SAW) has also offered Noon *(Dhor)* and Afternoon *(Asr)* as well as Evening *(Maghrib)* and Night *(Isha)* prayers together and therefore five times prayers could be also offered at three times in accordance with Ahl al-Bayt's (AS) School of Thought. [Tr]

according to strictly defined rules. Recommended prayers *(nawafil)* also follow the same pattern of ritual prayers but on the other hand, one may supplicate God any time in any circumstances without any set pattern or formulae; supplications are voluntary and informal and litanies and invocation i.e. the recitation of verses of the Holy Qur'an or one or more of God's names, like supplications are also optional. In order to attain higher spiritual stations and God's nearness, one should always be in a state of continuous ablution and invocations.

The present book deals with ritual prayer and describes its inner depths or profundities in a special manner; apart from its outer ritualistic format the prayer has inner mysteries of infinite sublime dimensions. It's like a fathomless ocean of infinite dimensions that one could utilize from it in accordance to his need or capacity. On the Day of Judgment the inhabitants of the hell would be asked: ***"What hath brought you to this burning? They will answer: 'We were not of those who prayed.'"***[1] The most important thing in prayer is sincerity, pure intentions, and presence of heart before God. The Holy Qur'an says: ***"Ah, woe unto worshippers, who are heedless of their prayer."***[2] Therefore, during performance of daily prayers, to control thoughts and to achieve presence of heart and mind strictly for God instead of getting occupied in worldly affairs is very crucial. It has been mentioned in the books written by most eminent Gnostics of our period like Imam Khomeini (RA), Grand Ayatollah Behjat (RA), Grand Ayatollah Maliki Tabrizi (RA), and others that God gives three chances to his servants during prayer; however if he still doesn't return towards Him after third chance, God turn his face away from the servant and his prayer is thrown upon his face. Unfortunately most of prayers don't go higher than roof of rooms, in which it's offered, but prayers offered with heart's presence and sincerity turns into illumination that goes up filtering through various heavens until it reaches near God.

If a person is submerged into love and desires of this glittering world and its charms, naturally his heart would be fully entangled

---

1. ***—The Holy Qur'an (74: 42-43).***
2. ***—The Holy Qur'an (107: 4-5).***

in nonsense affairs. So far the tree of love of worldly ambitions and desires has taken roots; heart would behave like bird jumping from branch to branch during prayer. If through struggle, practice, efforts, and thinking about severe consequences and losses, one could succeed in cutting the branches of this tree of worldly ambitions or desires, then heart would be become reposed and peaceful; it would then achieve the state of spiritual perfection. At least the more one tries to free himself from worldly charms, the more he succeeds in cutting various branches of that tree, the more presence of heart would be achieved proportionally. As far as the love of this world is concerned, there are people who don't possess any thing but still could be a person totally submerged into the love of this world. While on the contrary one might be like Prophet Solomon[1] (AS)—king of kings and possessing all treasures of this universe, but a the same time may not be a man of this world completely detached form the charms and love of this worldly existence.

It has been narrated in various authentic narrations that if one could offer only two units *(rak'ats)* of prayer in one's life time with complete devotion, sincerity, and presence of mind—God would accept it—and would bless His servant with Paradise. Regarding prostration it has been narrated that during one's entire life time if one succeeds during a single prostration to achieve a real union with the Creator—it would compensate for all of past omissions. He would receive divine blessing and would become immune from Satanic temptations forever. On the contrary if during prostration which is the state of complete renunciation—if his heart is still preoccupied with any thing other than God—he would be listed among the group of hypocrites and misled. One should seek refuge in God from the tricks of Satan and his own self, while in offering prayer and being in God's presence. In order to emphasize importance of prayer in linking a weak, helpless, poor, worthless, earthly creature with the most Supreme Source of Power, we may quote the following two authentic narrations as follows:

---

1. However, since he possessed this vast kingdom it's written in authentic narrations that he would be the last divine prophet to enter into paradise a distance equivalent to five hundred years. [Tr]

"God says [to His servant]: 'O my servant obey Me, so that I could make you like My Own Self.'"

—Mysteries of Prayer by
Grand Ayatollah Maliki Tabrizi (RA) page-4.

And the following:

"Through performance of optional (nawafil) prayers—my servant becomes so much nearer to Me that I start liking him. When this happens—I become his ears with whom he hears, become his eyes with who he sees, and become his hands with whom he does things …."

—Mysteries of Prayer by
Grand Ayatollah Maliki Tabrizi (RA) page-5.

The more one succeeds in achieving perfection in obedience of God—the more his acts would begin reflecting superior heavenly characteristics, and of course these stations of perfection and exaltation are achieved through being sincere in prayer which has been called as—prayer is the heavenly journey of a believer. One should know that in order to achieve the hearts presence one must be careful in making ablution for prayer. There are prayers from the Commander of Faithful, Imam Ali (AS) for washing the face, hands, wiping head and feet which should be recited during ablution. One should also think while washing his face that: ***"O God don't make it blackened on the Day of Judgment, while washing hands one should say: O God don't give my the report card of my deeds in my left hand instead give it in my right hand, and while wiping his hands and feet he should say: O God please make me under your obedience form head to feet, i.e. absolute surrender."***

He should also know that when he says the call of prayer, *(adhan)* and lesser call of prayer *(aghameh)* there would be two lines of angels offering prayer behind him—whose length would be equal to the distance between east and west or equivalent to the distance between earth and heaven. If he says only lesser call of *(aghameh)* prayer there would be one line of angles behind him offering the prayer. Therefore, if he doesn't have presence of heart and is submerged in worldly thoughts—it's something very shameful and disgusting indeed. When the servant recites the verse: ***"The (alone) we worship; the (alone) we ask for help,"*** while in reality he is thinking about other things then God says to him: ***"O liar, are you cheating Me?"***

Grand Ayatollah Qadhi the most exalted scholar and perfect Gnostic of his time in the religious Seminary of Najaf in Iraq has emphasized the importance of offering daily obligatory prayers at their exact times; he used to say that if you offer prayers at the right time and if you don't attained spiritual higher stations you may curse him. Grand Ayatollah Mohammad Ali Shahabadi the perfect Gnostic and honorable teacher of Gnosticism of—Imam Khomeini (RA) has also said that if you could offer prayers at exact times and practice not to lie—you would certainly attained higher spiritual stations. The Holy Prophet (SAW) has called prayer as the light of his eyes and used to say to his Announcer of the Call of prayer *(Moadhin)* Bilal at the time of prayers: ***"O Bilal make me comfortable (Arhana ya Bilal)."*** His color used to change at that time and he used to forget every thing at the time of prayer. There is a lot that could be written about importance of prayer but we would finish this forward with a beautiful and eloquent sermon delivered by Grand Ayatollah Sayyid Ali Khamenei—Supreme Leader of the I.R. Iran, the writer of this book on October 8, 1991 in Tehran as follows:

"There is no permanent and stronger link between men and God than prayer; the most elementary beginners start their relationship with God through the means of prayer. Also, the most important saintly personalities seek the paradise of solitude with their beloved during prayer. The treasure of remembrance and mysteries doesn't has limits; whoever makes sincere efforts and endeavors is accordingly blessed with more enlightenment. Our people, society, and especially youths who carry heavy load of trust upon their shoulders should consider prayer as an indestructible source of power. They must energize them with God's remembrance and prayer to stand against the forces of corruption, injustice,

and perverseness, which are threatening humanity today. The struggle we are facing today—more than ever and more than all others—makes us more dependent upon the powerful support of God's remembrance, and be hopeful and confident upon His help and support. The Prayer is such a fountainhead which bestows this hope, confidence, and spiritual strength upon us."

The present book consists of a preliminary introduction of importance of prayer in Islam. For more comprehensive studies readers should refer to the books: Etiquettes of Prayer and Mysteries of Prayer by Imam Khomeini (RA), and Mysteries of Prayer of Grand Ayatollah Maliki Tabrizi (RA). The book consists of eight chapters namely: Philosophy of prayer, Surah Opening *(al-Hamd)*, Surah Sincerity *(al-Ikhlas)*, Four Praises *(Tasbeeh Arba)*, Genuflection *(Rukoo)*, Prostration *(Sujood)*, Witnessing *(Tashahud)*, and Salutation *(Salam)*. I have tried to be loyal to the Persian text with best of my abilities; the notes added by the translator have been indicated by [Tr]. I am sincerely indebted to Ayatollah Ibrahim Amini, the learned scholar and jurisprudent from the Islamic Seminary of Qum for his sincere motivation and encouragement for translation of this work. I offer my sincere appreciation to Dr. Ali Naqi Baqershahi, of Ahl al-Bayt World Assembly for his encouragement and providing biography of Grand Ayatollah Sayyid Ali Khamenei. I apologize to my readers for possible errors, omissions and welcome their suggestions and comments.

Sayyid Hussein Alamdar,
Ahl al-Bayt (AS) Islamic Cultural Services (AICS) of USA.
alamdar_zaidi2000@yahoo.com
www.sayyidalamdar.com
www.amazon.com/author/sayyidalamdar
Rabi Al-Awaal 1437 A.H, Azar 24, 1394, December 15, 2015

***

Chapter-10: Philosophy of Prayer in Islam

Prayer and praise are most intimate communications between men and God, between the Creator and His creatures. Prayer bestows comfort and tranquility to exhausted, restless and disturbed hearts, and is the essence of inner purification and illumination for human soul. It's a commitment, motivation for action, mobilization, and announcement for readiness in a most sincere manner, far from any deceit or delusion, for negation of all kinds of wickedness, indecency, and affirmation of every goodness and beauty. It's a program for discovering self, and subsequently to build it up spiritually, or in nutshell, a continuous beneficial relationship with fountainhead of all goodness i.e. God. Why is prayer considered most important and prime obligation? Why has prayer been described as foundation and basis of faith? Why without prayer nothing will be acceptable? In order to find these answers, let us analyze and evaluate various dimensions and aspects of the prayer. To start with, it would be appropriate to focus on aims and objectives behind human creation, which is regarded as one of the main axis within the world view of Islamic ideology.

If men is a created being, and if we believe that a powerful and wise hand, brought him into being, then it's natural to think that there must be some aims and objectives behind this creation and existence. This aim may be called as, measuring, a road which leads to the final destination or God; traveling that road, according to the exact map and specified means, so as to eventually reach the desired final destination. In this case it's necessary to identify road which leads towards final destination, determine route, and always keep in mind the aim in order to achieve the desired result. One who starts this journey must walk straight ahead; should continuously keep in mind final destination; should not be distracted by diversions on the road; or loose attention to futile activities; also in order to continue, maintain correct position in specified direction, and not to deviate from the guidelines, prescribed by his leader i.e—the Holy Prophet SAW). That aim, is a step toward exaltation and infinite perfection by men. It's a return to God and to virtuous qualities. Discovering of inherent power and potential within himself; and utilizing of them on the righteous path, for his own welfare, fellow human beings, and the entire world. Therefore, we must identify existence of God, path prescribed by Him for exaltedness of human beings, and must move in that direction, without hesitation and lethargy.

To undertake works, which lead men closer to goal, disassociate with things which are injurious and harmful, and assign meaning to life, such should be the philosophy of life, otherwise its becomes useless without any content. In other words, life is like a class or laboratory, where we have to act in accordance with laws and formulas, which have been prescribed for us by God—the Creator of world and all life, in order to achieve and accomplish desired results. We must identify these laws, divine traditions, laws of creation, and mould our lives according to them. Therefore, one must first identify his own self, and its needs, which is regarded as one of great responsibilities and obligations of a human being. It's only after discharging of this great obligation that a human being would be able to move forward conscientiously with success, otherwise he would be regarded as an idle, ignorant, and a failure.

Religion not only determines goal, direction, ways and means of journey, but also bestows upon human beings necessary power, and provision for undertaking the journey on the road towards perfection. Of course, most important provision, which is carried by travelers on this road is nothing but God's remembrance. Powerful wings of this flight are quest, hope, and confidence, which are results of the same God's remembrance. On one hand it makes us aware of goal of attaching ourselves to Him—absolute perfection, and at the same time prevents deviations, and keeps traveler alert and cautious regarding ways and means. On the other hand, it bestows courage, happiness, and confidence upon him and protects him from distractions and frustrations when faced with harsh and adverse circumstances. Islamic society, and each group or individual, could move forward with certainty on this trail charted by Islam and blazed out by all divine prophets, without breaking the journey or returning from midway, only if they do not forget God's remembrance. Therefore, it's because of this consideration that religion tries its best, through suggesting various ways and means to keep alive God's remembrance in the believers' hearts at all times.

One such act, which is fully saturated with motivation of God's remembrance, and which enables men to submerge himself completely into it, makes him aware and self discovering, and acts as a signpost of straight course for those traversing God's path, prevents them from intricate passageways and blind alleys, and stands in the way of negligence—is nothing but prayer. Men, because of his preoccupations does not have opportunity to think or ponder about himself, on the aim of life, and about passage of moments, hours, and days. It's very often that days pass into nights, a new day begins, and weeks and months pass by without men having a chance to realize about passage of time, its meanings, and sheer waste. Prayer is like a siren for awakening, a warning at different hours of day and night, which provides a program for men, and requires his commitment for its execution, thus, bestowing meanings to days and nights and making him accountable for the passing moments. When men is immersed in his worldly affairs, without paying any attention to passage of time, and creeping of age, prayer summons him and makes him understand that a day has passed, and a new day has begun. He must act by assuming a greater responsibility by performing an important task, because a portion of life has already been spent. Therefore, one must try harder, and should take giant steps forward because the aim is lofty—till there is an opportunity, one should try to achieve it before it's too late.

On the other hand to forget goal and direction under pressures of day-to-day life or material involvement is a natural and obvious thing. Possibility to review all obligations assigned to men, in order to accomplish desired goal, during each day is rather difficult and almost impossible. In addition to that, sufficient time for reviewing

Islam's over all requirements and ideals, which bestow exaltedness and prosperity to human life, never exists and such an opportunity never arises. Prayer in itself contains the condensed summary of all principles of this school because the words, calculated and most organized harmonious movements which are contained in it, the prayer indeed may rightly be called as perfect and complete manifestation of Islam. Or, in other words, we may compare prayer with the national anthem of a country, of course with some difference in meanings and other parameters.

A country, in order to make its principles and ideals permanently recorded in minds and thoughts of its citizens, to keep alive their patriotism towards that ideology, composes a national anthem, containing a summary of those ideals, and makes its recital compulsory. Repeated recital of national anthem becomes a means, to make its citizens to remain committed to those ideals, as well as a reminder for them that they are citizens of that country and defenders of those ideals composed therein. Otherwise, forgetting those principles and ideals would mean, that they have deviated from them, and are no longer committed to them in their lives. Therefore, this repetition makes them ready and available for work and service for their country, teaches relevant methodology, assigns responsibilities and obligations, keeps alive principles in their minds, assists in their duties, and finally nurtures courage and power of action to discharge their duties successfully.

Like a national anthem for a country, prayer in nutshell is a total summary of Islamic ideology which explicitly defines path of a Muslim, and clearly indicates all responsibilities, obligations, ways, and results. It's the prayer which summons a Muslim at the beginning of a day, during mid day, at evening, and night, makes him understand principles, direction, goals, and results by his own tongue, encouraging him for action through bestowing upon him spiritual strength. It's prayer which step by step directs believer to reach peak of perfection, consisting of belief and action, and makes out of him a precious object i.e. an ideal perfect Muslim. It's because of these characteristics that the Holy Prophet (SAW) has called the prayer: ***"A ladder of believer carrying him higher up towards heavens."***

Men has a difficult and lengthy road ahead of him, which leads him towards real righteousness and prosperity. To travel on this road of perfection has been primordial aim of men's creation and existence. But what he is confronted with, is not this single road alone, rather he has to avoid obscure and narrow lanes, diversions, and dangerous paths that abound just near the main straight road. Sometimes these paths are so tempting and full of attractions that a traveler becomes easily confused and selects the wrong route by mistake.

Therefore, to avoid these pitfalls, a traveler has to stick to original program i.e. to ascertain correct direction, and march forward towards cherished aim and ultimate destination—movement towards God, through following prescribed map showing path, and goal. Prayer is nothing other than a constant attention towards God and a detailed map showing the main path. It's a channel providing a permanent contact and firm link with God because it contains a complete summary of Islamic thoughts in its rituals. With the above discussion, it therefore becomes explicit that what is the reason behind prescribing prayers five times a day and to what extent it's crucial? It may be compared like the food requirement of human body at different intervals during a twenty four hour period.

Apart from the fact that prayer contains a total summary of all Islamic aims and ideals, and since recital of the Holy Qur'an is compulsory during its rituals, naturally prayer makes individual performing it familiar with a portion of the Holy Qur'an's text, and thus encourages him to ponder and think about its meanings which gradually becomes his habit. The movements which are prescribed in the prayer are a complete and total reflection of Islam in a miniature form. In a social system, Islam incorporates body, mind, and soul of human beings and puts them to work to produce prosperity and happiness for them. Same thing is accomplished exactly when one offers prayers, because all three namely: body, mind, and soul are put to work and involvement as follows:

Body: The hands, feet, and tongue, are all in motion as prayer requires three postures of standing, genuflection, and prostration.

Mind: Thinking about contents and wordings of prayer which normally is an indication about aims and means; and it's like the completion of a short course about the method of thinking in Islamic ideology.

Soul: God's remembrance, and spiritual flight towards sublime higher plains, through cutting all worldly adventures of heart into numerous nonsense and amusements, and trying to achieve presence of heart through concentration, as well as to nourish seeds of humility and fear of God in a human being's soul.

It's an accepted fact that prayer of each religion or ideology reflects a condensed summary of that particular school of thought. Similar is true with prayer in Islam i.e. it combines, soul, and body, material and meanings, world and hereafter, in words, context, and in motion which is specialty of prayer in Islam. A Muslim through offering a complete prayer could utilize all his own energy for achieving exaltation i.e. simultaneously he commissions all physical and spiritual resources towards this end. A believer offering prayer, seeking God's path with total physical and mental power concentration succeeds in overcoming all motives of wickedness, corruption and degradation, making himself immune from all sorts of evil influences. Some of the Holy Qur'an's verses describe establishment of prayer as a sign of religiousness, while many other verses put special emphasize for this act. Therefore, it seems that establishment of prayer goes further deeper than simply offering prayer. It's not sufficient for a believer to simply offer his own prayer, rather he is also responsible to endeavor for accomplishing aims, goals, and follow the path prescribed by it for him, as well as encouraging others to accompany him in that direction. In other words, it seems that offering means that one must do his utmost endeavor for establishment of God-seeking and God-worshipping environment for himself and others, moving community collectively forward in the direction of prayer.

A believer, or a society of believers through establishing prayer burns the roots of deviations, sins, and corruptions within themselves and their social environments, as well as at the same time neutralizes completely all kind of sinful thoughts and internal and external motives of wickedness be individual or collective, whatsoever. Certainly prayer protects individual as well as a society from all sorts of undesirable and shameful acts. During the crucial struggle of life, when devilish forces are completely equipped and mobilized for destruction of all motives and stimulants of goodness and righteousness within everybody and everywhere, the prime castle which is attacked and destroyed by them consists of men's determination and spiritual strength. Because once this dignified barrier is removed, occupation and destruction of the castle representing human personality—a castle which is treasure of all inherent nobilities, and accumulation of precious learning and knowledge—becomes possible. Therefore, those who proclaim a fresh and novel message for their period are attacked much more severely, and require intensely to defend this irresistible fortification relatively more than others.

Prayer of Islam through inspiration and repetition of God's remembrance connects limited and vulnerable men to unlimited and absolute power, and makes him rely upon that source. Through linking human being to that absolute power, and manager of all universes, bestows upon him infinite and indestructible power, which could be regarded as the most ideal treatment for his weakness and effective medicine inducing determination and strong will. The Holy Prophet (SAW) at the threshold of great resurrection of Islam, and facing total confrontation with pagans, felt heaviest burden of obligations and responsibilities upon his shoulders, was instructed by God to offer midnight prayers, *(namaz-e-shab or salatul lail)* and praise of God as follows:

"O! Thou wrapped up in thy raiment! Keep vigil the night long, save a little. A half thereof, or abate a little thereof. Or add (a little) thereto and chant the Qur'an in measure. For We shall charge thee with a word of weight."

—The Holy Qur 'an (73: 1-5).

Now, we would review contents of prayer in a manner without going deep into an expanded translation or interpretation. Efforts will be made to lead the readers one step closer to the aim of prayer. Prayer begins with the Name of God and with remembrance of its glory, the unlimited extent of His essence, and its absolute domination and superiority from the highest point of men's thinking:

"God is Great (Allah ho Akbar)."

A believer starts his praise with the above sentence, and for a magnificent act, starts an opening chapter saturated with splendor. God is Great—greater than, whatever could be confined into virtues or qualities. Greater than to be compared with proclaimers of divinity and god ling throughout the history, and greater than all the powers and natural displays and appearance of which men might be afraid or may be tempted for, and greater than anybody who could dare to challenge His divine and creational laws. If a God's servant has already recognized these divine traditions, in accordance to them has selected path, and endeavors in that direction, then with this reminder that God is Greatest, gets a tremendous power with in his existence and becomes fully saturated with hope. With complete assurance he knows that all his efforts have been successful and eventually the end is going to be well. These assurances make him hopeful and satisfied regarding the path he has selected looking ahead for the bright future. After announcing this sentence the worshiper practically enters into the ritual of prayer. He must recite the Surah Praise or Opening *(al-Hamd)* and there after one complete Surah from the Holy Qur'an in the standing position.

Chapter-11: Surah The Opening *(Al-Hamd)*

In the Name of God the Beneficent, the Merciful ***(Bismil-laahir-Rahmanir-Raheem)*** in the name of God, who is possessor of all blessings and everlasting compassion. The above sentence which is first sentence of all Surahs of the Holy Qur'an[1] is the opening of prayer, as well as beginning of all activities and involvements of a Muslim i.e. all works begin only with the Name of God, everything belonging to a human being—the beginning of his life, as well as all manifestations of his being alive are in His name. A Muslim starts his days and terminates his daily endeavors, closes his eyes permanently from this world to become the part of eternity.

"Praise be to God, Lord of the Worlds (Alhamdulillahe Rabbil Aalameen)." [2]

All praise and thanks belong specially to Him, because He is the source of all Greatness and Blessings. He is assembly of all praiseworthy characteristics, all goodness, and righteousness which oases from the fountainhead of His essence.

---

1. Except the ninth Surah i.e. Surah Repentance *(Touba)* or Immunity *(Barr'at).*

2. The Opening *(Al-Fatihah)*, or The Opening of the Scripture *(Fatihatu'l-Kitab)* or The Essence of the Qur'an *(Ummul-Qur'an)*, as it's variously named, has been called the Lord's Prayer of Muslims. It's an essential part of all Muslim worship, public and private. This surah is also mentioned as: ***"We have given thee seven of the oft-repeated (verses) and the great Qur'an."***

—The Holy Qur 'an (15: 87).[Tr]

Therefore, God's praise means praise of all goodness and righteous deeds. He is one who assigns direction or purpose to all efforts supporting goodness and righteousness. If we observe some praiseworthy characteristics and manners in ourselves, we must consider them as a kindness, favor, and blessing from God. Because God has actually incorporated potential for goodness within human nature, and prepared his essence in such a way that he is always seeking excellence. Also He bestowed upon men power of self determination as another instrument for performance of the righteous and noble deeds. This God given insight not only closes door for becoming a self centered and self-conceited being, but also at the same time prevent wastage and improper utilization of virtuosity and creative potentials within human nature. The sentence Lords of worlds describes existence of other worlds and gives a feeling that all these universes and galaxies are interrelated together and forms a single unit.

Thus, a believer discovers that apart from this world, and his limited and narrow vision beyond the boundaries imagined by him for his life, there exists other celestial spheres, universes, galaxies, and God is also the Lord of all this magnificent vast kingdom. This realization, therefore destroys all sort of narrow mindedness and shortsightedness feelings and bestows upon him courage and a sense of search. Servitude to God creates a special feeling of pride within him, and through becoming a God's servant, he discovers a special magnificence and splendor around him. Looking from a different angle he will discover that all creatures, namely human beings, animals, plants, stationary objects, skies, and numerous galaxies of the universe, all are in absolute servitude to God, Who is their Lord and manages the whole universe.

He understands that his God is not only God of his race, his country, and mankind, but also, belongs to that tiny ant and weak plant as well. He is also God of heavens, milky ways, and stars. With this realization he discovers that he is not alone, rather is related with all tiny particles or large creatures of this universe. He is associated and interrelated with all human kinds, all of them are brothers and fellow-travelers, and this great caravan of humanity is heading for a single goal. This awareness of association, interrelation, and connection makes him obliged and committed with respect to all creatures. Regarding mankind he is responsible for showing commitments, guidance, and assistances; while with respect to other creatures, he is committed to their proper identification, and utilization in a proper way in accordance with divine aim and direction.

"The Beneficent, the Merciful (Al-Rahma nir Rahim)."

God's general blessing in the from of creative powers, life giving laws, and sources of continuous energies created for the support of universe, surrounds all creatures, and everything and everyone till the last moment requires this blessing or beneficence. On the other side, His special blessing—blessing for guidance and assistance, for rewarding, and affection—belongs to His righteous and pious servants. This special merciful blessing like a lighting route becomes a part of existences of these precious and decent creatures and remains with them until death, and from death until resurrection and final eternal abode. Thus, God bestows general blessing, which belongs to all but is temporary, and a special blessing belonging to special groups which is permanent and forever. Therefore, the remembrance of merciful virtues of God, in the Holy Qur'an's preface for beginning of prayer, and at each Surah indicates that affection and benevolence of God is in abundance and more conspicuous at the scene of creation as compared to His wrath and punishment, which is reserved only for enemies, obstinate, corrupters and criminals; while his blessing surrounds everything all around.[1]

---

1. ***"And ordain for us in this world that which is good, and in the hereafter (that which is good). Lo! We have turned into Thee. He said: I smite with My punishment whom I will, and My mercy embraces all things, therefore I shall ordain it for those who ward off (evil) and pay the poor-due, and those who believe in Our revelations."***

—The Holy Qur'an (7: 156).

"Thou whose mercy overtakes your wrath!"

—The prayer Maasoor.

"Owner of the Day of Judgment (Malike Yaumiddeen)."

The day of resurrection, is ultimate conclusion of our actions during our worldly lives. We try our best to have a good end, and aspire to achieve best conclusions. In this struggle both materialist without God, and those who believe in God, all in their endeavors search for achieving a good end ultimately. The difference consists that each one has its own interpretation about the conclusion. For a materialist ultimate end means, next hour, next day, next year or next few years, and ultimately getting old and depreciated with the passage of time, but from the point of view of a believer in God, ultimate consequences mean much deeper and farther than described above. From a believer's point of view world is not confined to limited boundaries, rather his future is unlimited which raises within him infinite hope encouraging him for working hard without ever getting exhausted. Such a person who never gives up hope for getting rewarded, and seeing results of his deeds even after dying may continue his goodly deeds for the sake of God's pleasure with excitement till the very last moment of his life.

The reminder that God is absolute owner, and all commands belongs to Him on the Day of Resurrection, bestows an ability upon the person who is offering prayer to walk in the right direction, and makes all his actions and efforts oriented in God's direction. Life and all manifestations for being alive becomes for the sake of God and His path. Everything belonging to him and all his efforts and actions are utilized in the direction of perfection and excellence of mankind the only direction pleasing to God. On the other hand, door of reliance upon false imaginations and unrealistic expectations is closed upon him, and true hopes for action are induced within his inner existence. If in this world, wrong systems and deviated corrupt regimes have provided opportunities for lazy minded elements to be able to engage in plunder and usurpation, without taking any pains or making efforts by simply utilizing deceptions, lies, and fraudulent tactics; in the next world where all efforts are managed and controlled strictly by a wise and just God, such fraud and cheating would be impossible, and no one would be rewarded for things in which he has not participated.

Here the first half of Surah Praise *(al-Hamd)* which contains glorification of the Lord of Worlds, and describes some qualities of His essence reaches to its completion. The second half portion which consists of acceptance of servitude, bondage, and need for guidance throws light upon some very important principles of Islamic ideology.

"Thee (alone) we worship; Thee (alone) we ask for help (Iyyaka Nabudu Waiyyaka Nastaeen)."

All physical, spiritual, and mental abilities of our existence are at God's disposal, and are ready for His command and in his direction. The person who offers prayer through declaring this sentence breaks chain of bondage from other than God, and frees his hands, feet, and neck, and therefore rejects claims of false deities—the arrogant claimers of divinity—who have always been responsible for the creation of upper and lower classes in a society throughout the history, and made the majority of mankind oppressed, deprived, and kept them into chains of slavery. The one who offers prayer takes himself as well as all other believers in God, further away from the limits of obedience and servitude of anybody other than God, and any system than divine government. In summary, through accepting God's servitude throws away the servitude of other fellow creatures, and through doing so joins the rank of real disciples of the School of Monotheism. Admittance and acceptance to the fact that bondage and servitude is permissible only in front of God and only for Him, is one of the most important principle, theoretical as well as practical, of Islamic ideology, and all other divine religions; which means that divinity or providence belongs exclusively to God, i.e. only He has the right to be worshipped and there is no god but God, and therefore, nobody other than Him should be praised or worshipped.

Unfortunately there were some people whose interpretation was incorrect and limited, could not understand its meanings properly, and therefore unknowingly become prey to the servitude of other than God. They imagined that God's worship is limited only to praising and adoring Him, and since they offered prayers in the sight of God and only praised Him, through doing so they become convinced that they had worshipped no one other than God. The knowledge of the comprehensive meaning of worship from the point of view of the Holy Qur'an and traditions would clarify the baseless ness of the above mentioned interpretation. In accordance with the Holy Qur'an's terminology and traditions, worship may be defined as: Obedience, surrender, and absolute submission to commands, regulations, and codes issued from the holder of authority or center of power, and are imposed upon mankind whether this submission and obedience is accompanied by a sense of praise sanctification or otherwise.

Therefore, in accordance with above definition, all of those who have surrendered to regulations, codes, and commands issued by any power other than God become it's worshippers, bondsmen, and manifestations. In spite of that, if there is still some room left for following the divine commands, and in some parts or some areas in their individual or social lives, they obey divine laws and ordinances—they will be called as polytheists, i.e. those who in addition to worshipping God also worship some others. And if nothing is left for God, they are called unbelievers i.e. those who do not see the most visible and brilliant reality about divine existence and deny it in their beliefs and actions. With above Islamic reasoning, it may be easily understood that why in all divine religions the sentence—there is no god but God[1]—was their prime slogan. This reality—the reality of meanings of prayer—in Islamic documents, in the Holy Qur'an, and in traditions have been mentioned repeatedly and explicitly, so that for thinkers and intellectuals there should not remain least possibility for contradiction or doubt. As an example, we will refer to the following two verses of the Holy Qur'an and a tradition quoted by Imam J'afar al-Sadiq (AS) as follows:

"They have taken as lords beside God, their rabbis and their monks and the Messiah son of Marry, when they were bidden to worship only One God. There is no god save Him. Be He glorified from all that they ascribe as partner (unto Him)."

—The Holy Qur'an (9:31).

---

[1] Refer to the Holy Qur'an Surah Al-A'raf verses 59 till 158, Surah Hud verses 50 till 84, where the slogan has been proclaimed by some of great divine prophets.

"And those who put away false gods lest they should worship them and turn to God in repentance, for them there are glad tidings. Therefore, give good tidings (O Muhammad) to my bondmen."

—The Holy Qur'an (39:17).

Zumar Abu basir narrates following narration from Imam J'afar al-Sadiq (AS), who addressed to the real Shi'i of his period:

"You are the ones who have refused to worship false deities. And whoever has obeyed command of a despot or tyrant has indeed worshipped him."[1]

"Thee (alone) we worship; Thee (alone) we ask for help (Iyaaka n'ab do wa iyyaka nastaeen)."

We do not expect any kind of help or support from your rivals and claimers of divinity. Because of their denial to accept God's divinity, they can not be of any help for seekers and followers of God's path, followed by divine prophets, is a source for accomplishing truth, justice, brotherhood, and co-existence for mankind. It bestows exaltedness upon human beings, while condemning and negating all sort of prejudices, oppressions, and unequal treatments or preferences shown towards a certain class or group. How God's rivals, claimers of divinity who are devoted entirely to this shameful worldly existence, and through their usurping behavior have not left any stone unturned in their efforts to destroy all real human values, could be of any help to God's bondsmen? They are at permanent war and carry a burning wrath against God's bondsmen, and believers. Therefore, we only seek help from God; the power of intellect and decision making, incorporated through Him in our primordial nature; ways and means provided for living this life; natural and historical laws, which if could be understood may act as a guide for our thoughts and actions; and also from all byproducts of divine power which are His mighty soldiers in the service of mankind.

---

1. *Tafseer Noor-al-Thaqalain,* v. 5, p-481, also refer to verse 17 of Surah Zumar.

"Show us the straight path (Ehdinas siratal mustqeem)."

If men could have a superior and more vital matter of life and death, aim and objective than guidance certainly that would have been included in Surah Praise—a Surah which is the opening chapter of the Holy Qur'an and forms an important part of prayer—and it would have been recited as a prayer for acceptance from God. It's by way of His direction or guidance, that intellect and experience set their course in the correct, advantageous, and suitable position, widening the path of wayfarer. Otherwise, without it, intellect and experience would turn into a light in the hands of a thief, or a piece of sharp blade in the hand of a mad man. The straight path is same primordial destined program, which has been prepared in accordance with most accurate estimation regarding available sources, needs, and shortages within bounds of natural possibilities for mankind. It's a path opened towards humanity by God's prophets who themselves were pioneer searchers and wayfarers on this path. The path if followed by men could be analogized like a continuous streamlined flow of water over a smooth and straight surface, which by itself and without any interference, showing any force or power is flowing towards final destination, which is nothing but infinite ocean of human exaltedness.

It's a program if could be implemented and materialized under a just administration to manage people's lives, will provide independence, security, benefits, cooperation, self sufficiency, love, brotherhood, and will bring an end to all bitter accidents and tragedies associated with mankind in their past. But what is this path and program supposed to be? Every one in this amazed bazaar is a claimer and each group condemns the other. Therefore there must be an indication, in accordance with this brief preface, regarding this straight path, and to specify it from the point of view of Holy Qur'an:

"The path of those whom Thou hast favored (Siratal lazeena anamta alaihim)."

Who were the people able to receive rewards from God and were blessed with special favors? There is no doubt that this does not mean material prosperity, position, and power. Because these were things possessed by most prominent personalities of history, who at the same time were worst enemies of God and people. Therefore, those desired favors and blessing must be something far deeper than these worldly attractions. That blessing is special favor, grant, and guidance of God. The blessing of recognition of real value of self and to discover again the inner self. The Holy Qur'an describes that special blessing: ***"Whoso obeyeth God and the messenger, they are with those unto whom God hath shown favor, of the Prophets and the saints and the martyrs and the righteous.[1] The best of the company are they!"***

—The Holy Qur'an (4: 69).

Thus, the one who offers prayer in this sentence requests for guidance towards the path of divine prophets, saints, martyrs, and righteous men. The main illuminated path of history, a clear visible path with fully defined and determined aims with famous and well known searchers. Opposite to this, there is another well defined path with its wayfarers completely identified. Keeping this in mind the one who offers prayer warns himself not to follow that path and in continuation of his early recitation, recites the following:

"Not (the path) of those who earn Thine anger (Ghairil maghdhoobe alaihim)."

Who were the people received God's wrath? Those who decided to follow the path other than God's not only they selected this wrong path, but were able to lead with themselves by force a group of ignorant, indecisive, lazy people, and also some aware and determined people, but with their hands chained into captivity, to follow that path. These were people, who all along the history succeeded to control the state of affairs of masses. Sometimes it was achieved by use of brute force or at other times through using dirty tricks, demagogy, and cheating. The aim was to force masses to become like indecisive creatures or like a mere tool oppressed into

1. Those who proved and confined their belief by their actions and deeds and thus were able to witness God and His prophets.

the hands of oppressors and tyrants. Those were people, who, through ways of infatuation superimposed themselves upon masses and thus succeeded to possess resources for their corrupt and filthy pleasure seeking passionate affairs. In other words, these people selected the path of evil not because of ignorance, but they rebelled knowingly for the sake of their selfish passion.

The historical realities show that religious objectives always took pioneer steps to demonstrate against the worldly, powerful, wealthy, upper classes, and rejected the philosophy of their existence because it was in conflict with religious aims and objectives. Apart from these two groups, i.e. the one who received God's guidance, and the one who earned His wrath, there exists another third group, who followed eventually the same path followed by the latter group.[1] The last sentence of Surah Praise defines this third group as follows:

"Nor of those who go astray (Waladhdhaaleen)."

Those, who because of their ignorance, and under the influence of misguided leaders, selected the path other than God's and truth, but imagined that had selected the righteous and straight path. While in reality they were walking on a dangerous misleading path, eventually leading to a bitter and doomful end. Let us look upon this above-mentioned group in the historical retrospective. These are people who under the pagan systems, hand folded and blindly allowed themselves at complete disposal of their misguided, deviated leaders, and for the sake of their advantages stood up against the divine messengers—proclaimers of truth and justice—thus, damaging their positions; and in doing so, they never allowed themselves to ponder over even for an instant to rethink about their foolish acts.

Their above acts could be called unwise or foolish, because they were totally to the advantages of upper classes and on the contrary losses for these deviated ones; just opposite to the invitation

[1]. This topic has been described with a style full of meanings at different occasions in the following verses of the Holy Qur'an: Surah Poets, verses 91-102; Surah Ibrahim, verses 21-22; Surah Saad, verses 58-61; al-Mu'min, verses 47-48.

of divine prophets, which was beneficial and useful for deprived masses including these deviated ones, while at the same time it destroyed existence and prestige of disfavored people from the roots. The worshipper through remembering these two alternative methodologies or paths i.e. the path of guided ones and the path of disfavored ones, must search within his inner self, and should decide with care, accuracy, and sensitivity the path he must follow and the stand which should be taken by him towards the life-saving message of the divine prophets. Thus at that moment through witnessing signs of maturity and guidance of God in his own life, once again opens his tongue for offering his thanks and gratefulness for that great blessing of God through saying (at the end of Surah Praise) as follows:

"Praise be to God, Lords of the worlds (Al-hamdu llilahe Rabbilaalameen)." [1]

And in this way he completes an important part of his prayer. This was preface of the Holy Qur'an and is also called opening of the scripture *(fathihatul-kitab)*. The Holy Qur'an's preface like preface of each book indicates overall essence of total content of the Holy scripture. As prayer is a summary or bird's-eye view picture of Islam, and represents many of prominent parameters or dimensions of Islamic ideology; likewise Surah The Opening lists prominent points and real direction of Qur'an's education and in nutshell contains the summary of important guide-lines in the following manner:

Universe and all creatures or species are one single unit—totally created by God—the Lord of worlds. Everybody and everything are under God kindness and affection. But the believers are blessed with special favors and mercies of God—the Beneficent and the Merciful. The life of men after this world continues and exists into hereafter, where absolute authority belongs to God—***"The Owner of the Day of Judgment."*** Men should free himself from bondage of other than God's. Should endeavor to live under the shadow of God's plan with determination and human virtues, upon the path, with freedom and dignity and get help only from Him—***"Thee alone***

1. The recital of this sentence is optional.

we worship, Thee alone we ask for help." Men must seek program for prosperity and success for walking upon the straight path of life from God—***"Show us the straight path."*** Must identify front lines of enemies and friends, should be aware about their views and positions. Should take a conscientious choice about his own path i.e. ***"The path of those Thee hast favored; not (the path) of those who earn Thine anger nor of those who go astray."***

Chapter-12: Surah The Sincerity *(al-Ikhlas)*

After recital of this Surah Praise which is full of deep learning and meanings the worshipper must recite another one complete Surah from the Holy Qur'an. This refreshes his memory for a part of the Holy scripture selected by his own choice and freewill, or in other words it opens another chapter of the Islamic learning in front of him. Obligation of recital of the Holy Qur'an during prayer has been explained in a narration quoted by Imam Ali bin Musa al-Rida (AS). Imam told to Fazl bin Shazan that recital of Surahs of the Holy Qur'an during prayer has prevented the Holy scripture from becoming abandoned, not comprehensively understood, and has kept its contents alive in thoughts and minds. In our discussion it will be sufficient to discuss Surah Sincerity *(Al-Ikhlas)*[1] which is normally recited in the prayer after recital of Surah Praise.

"In the Name of God, the Beneficent, the Merciful (Bismil-laahir- Rahmanir-Raheem)."

"Say: He is God, the One (Qul huwal-laahu Ahad)!" [2]

Unlike gods of deviated ideologies of other religions, He does not have any partners rivals, or equivalents. It means creation is free

1. The Sincerity *(Al-Ikhlas)*, also known as *Al-Tawhid,* takes its name from its subject. It has also been called the essence of the Holy Qur'an. Some authorities ascribe this Surah to the Medina period, and think that it was received in answer to a question of some Jewish doctors concerning God's nature. It's generally held to be an early Meccan Surah. [Tr]

2. The one God, the unique God. Therefore, the pronoun He is used and recited for the dignity.

of conflict and war between different gods. Rather, all traditions and laws of the universe are raised from one source of external power, through a single decision. It's because of this force that a coordinated discipline, and homogeneity is maintained through the universe. All laws, transformations, and natural motions of universe are moving in one single direction towards one single goal. Among all of them only men have been given the power of decision and right of determination. He is capable to disobey this divine discipline, and may play a music, in conflict and uncoordinated with other musical instruments, or may sing a melody like a lone singer. Also, he is capable to select to live his life in accordance with these divine commands.

"God the eternally, Besought of all (Allaahus-Samad)!"

God is free from everybody and everything, God to whom we adore, praise, and pay homage is not like imaginary gods whose creation, continuity of lives, strength, and living require help, support, and favor of someone else. Such a god is creature equivalent to men or meeker or a little lower. Men—this magnificent deep creature—will surrender himself, and adore and praise only a supreme power, which does not require least want from any other source or element. His being existed, powerful, and eternal all depend upon his own essence.

"He begetteth not (Lam yalid)."

It's not so! The way it has been ridiculously imagined among deviated religions or polytheist dogmas. He is not like imagined god of Christians and Polytheists who could be father of a son. He is One, who creates everything and everyone—and is not their father. All creatures of this universe be heavenly or earthly are his servants—and not his sons or daughters. It's because of this special relationship bondage vs. divinity between men and God, which frees the real servants of Him from slavery of everything and everybody. Because a servant simultaneously could not be owned by two masters. Those who imagined God as kind father of men and other creatures and did not consider relationship bondsman vs. divinity between men and God as something worthy enough for men's exalted position; in reality opened for themselves the door for bondage of other than God;

and in doing so become slaves of many of unkind slave-owners of this world, through turning into handpicked tools and possessions of slave-owners and slave producers.

"Nor was begotten (Wa lam yoolad)."

He is not phenomenon, which did not exist one day, and would become visible in the world of existence next day. He neither is physically begotten by anyone nor he is by-product of someone's thought or imaginations. Neither He is produced by a superior military force or super class, nor He resembles with any form of human life. He is supreme and most esteemed reality an eternal One, which existed before and will exist forever.

"And there is none comparable unto Him (Wa lam yakul laahu kufooaan ahad)."

He could not be compared to anyone or anything and no one could be found as His rival or equivalent. It's not possible to divide domain of His influence or His kingdom, which includes entire universe, between Him and someone else i.e. to consider a part of the world or portion of human life belongs to God and remaining belonging to someone other than Him. Or to allocate a part of universe and stage of human life between Him and others; between gods of alive and gods of dead; or to assign them to false claimers of godhood and power. As the name indicates this Surah is in reality the Surah of Monotheism. The philosophy of Monotheism, which has been explained in various tones and different styles, in hundreds of Surahs throughout the Holy Qur'an; in this Surah, has been presented in a condensed form and clear cut manner which overrides prevalent ridiculous and Polytheistic thinking of that period denying and negating explicitly all claimers of false godhood for the last time in the Holy scripture's text. This Surah introduces God's characteristics, which from Islamic point of view deserves to be praised and worshipped not only by Muslims, but by entire mankind living in His kingdom.

A god who is not unique, and hundreds and thousands of his look-alike are in abundance among mankind, is not deserving of divinity or godhood. A powerful person or a source of power, requiring help and support of other source for his continuation or existence does not deserve, and should not be imposed upon mankind. The one, who lowers his head in front of a puppet god, a created being, needy, and fallible has indeed shamed, lowered human dignity, and has taken a backward step. This is positive dimension of Surah of Monotheism or Sincerity, which indicates and distinguishes the characteristics of the Lords of Worlds, and simultaneously negates the existence of puppet gods throughout the history.

On the other hand this Surah warns Monotheistic worshippers and Muslim believers, not to be curious and indulgent into mental, rational debates regarding God's characteristics and essence, which would lead them to doubts and evil temptations rather they should seek and remember God by short words in order to get rid of false claimers of divinity and from their idle talks. Instead of getting trapped into philosophical puzzling they should ponder over commitments arising out of Monotheistic belief. According to a tradition, narrated by Imam Ali bin al-Hussein (AS), since God was aware that later period of history, would produce curious people, and therefore He revealed the verses of Surah Iron[1] till the verse: ***"Knower of all that is in the***

---

[1] Surah: Iron *(al-Hadid)* takes its name from a word in v. 25. The reference in the word victory in the verse 10 is undoubtedly to the conquest of Mecca, though Noldeke takes it to refer to the battle of Badr and so would place the Surah in the forth or fifty year of migration. The words of verse are against such an assumption since no Muslim spent and fought before the Battle of Badr, which was beginning of their fighting. The date of revelation must be eighth or ninth year of the migration. The first six verses of this Surah referred in the above discussion are as follows:

"In the Name of God, the Beneficent, the Merciful

1. All that is in the heavens and on the earth glorifieth God; and He is the Mighty; the Wise.

2. His is the Sovereignty of the heavens and the earth; He quickeneth and He gives death; and He is able to do all things.

breasts," in order to define boundaries for investigating His essence and characteristics. Therefore whosoever has allowed himself to ponder over beyond these prescribed limits is bound to be doomed.

As if this Surah—say God is One—says to the worshipper: God is unique supreme power, the most high, exalted, and needless. His Essence is beyond description, neither begets nor begotten, and there is no one similar to Him or His equivalent. Learned, seer, wise..... etc., and other characteristics of God's essence whose knowledge and awareness is obligatory for Muslims, and are regarded influential and effective in shaping their lives, and ascension of their spirits, have been repeated in the Holy Qur'an's other Surahs. Do not think beyond limits as already defined in this surah about God's essence and know-how about His characteristics. Rather, concentration should be exerted for performing deeds, which would eventually enlighten the believer in knowing God better. Do not think that through engaging in lengthy mental debates about His essence you will achieve more enlightenment. It's not so! Instead, try to achieve this desired enlightenment through bringing purification and spirituality to your inner self, and practicing principles of Monotheism in your deeds and actions; and that is the way the divine prophets, saints, God's righteous servants, pure Monotheists, and Gnostics were.

3. He is the First and the Last, and the Outward and the Inward; and He is the Knower all things.

4. He it is Who created the heavens and the earth in six Days; then He mounted the Throne. He knoweth all that entereth the earth and all that emergeth therefrom and all that cometh down from the sky and all that ascendeth therein; and He is with you whosesoever ye may be. And God is the seer of what ye do.

5. His is the Sovereignty of the heavens and the earth. and unto God (all) things are brought back.

6. He causeth the night to pass into the day, and He causeth the day to pass into the night, and He is Knower of all that is in the breasts." [Tr]

Chapter-13: Four Praises *(Tasbihatul-Arba)*

Before discussing hymns and special praises offered during genuflection and prostration, we will discuss phrases recited in the third and fourth units of prayer in the standing state. These phrases consist of recital of four invocations *(dhikr)*, describing four realities about God:

"Glory to God! (Subhan Allahi).

All praises belong to God (Wal hamdu lillahi).

And there is no god but God (Wa la ilahi illallahu).

And God is Great (Wallahu Akbar)."

Awareness regarding above four divine characteristics helps a lot, and has a tremendous influence about the correct and complete understanding of Monotheism, because each one of above indicates one body and one facade of the Monotheistic structure. The aim behind repetition of above sentences of praises is not only to increase mental enlightenment, or knowledge, rather understanding of divine characteristics and their continuous repetition, produces a sense of responsibility, whereby one would discharge all duties and obligations paramount to the reality discovered by him. Overall, apart from mental boundaries, Islamic beliefs are supposed to provide motivation for action in real life. Because irrespective of their theoretical mental dimensions, they are accredited in Islam, for playing a crucial role in supervising human lives in individual as well as collective social actions of a society. It's true, that each Islamic belief means recognition of a certain reality but only those beliefs in Islam are made mandatory that in case of their acceptance and adherence it would initiate a commitment for men through assigning an additional responsibility upon his shoulders.

That is the way belief about God's existence supposed to be. Belief in God's existence or non-existence, each one in a special way, brings new options for action in life. Individual or society if indeed believes in God's existence spends its life in a special manner other than those who denies this reality. If men believed that he and this universe have been created by a supreme source of power based upon His wisdom and knowledge; then he has no choice but to accept that this creation has some purpose and ultimate goal. Thus, he realizes that he too has an important role to play, and is supposed to assume certain responsibility, for accomplishing that aim. This awareness of commitment and responsibility motivates him for making endeavor by accepting higher burden, and in doing so he feels happy and satisfied.

Likewise belief in resurrection, prophet hood, and leadership of the Infallible Imams *(Vilayat)* etc each one carries a commitment and assign a burden of heavy responsibility upon the shoulders of a believer, and in totality the path, program, and overall direction of life are made distinguished for him. If outwardly it appears that those who believe in these ideological principles, and those who are completely ignorant or do not believe at all, are living an identical and similar lives without least problem or conflict—is due to the fact that the former group lacks the correct understanding—the degree of their faith is not sound, and do not believe the way it's supposed to be. At sensitive moments and critical junctures of life the path of real believers separates from the ignorant followers, opportunists and pseudo-believers. Keeping these views in mind we return to discuss the substance and content of above-mentioned Four Praises *(Tasbihatul-Arba)* as follows:

"Glory to God (Subhan Allahi)."

God is Holy, free from being associated with someone, from tyranny or oppression, from being created, from doing things against wisdom and advice, from all deficiencies and defects, and all filth which exists among created beings and all those characteristics associated with them. Through reciting this sentence the worshipper understands and reminds himself that against what kind of grand-magnificent power—worthy of praise—he has surrendered himself and offered prostration. He realizes that he has humbled himself before a power which is a source of righteousness and absolute perfection. Is it possible that someone who has respected the source of absolute perfection of all goodness, righteousness, and beauty will feel contempt for it? This is what the prayer of Islam is supposed to be. It's to show humility and respect in front of an existence which is like an infinite ocean of perfections good nesses and manifestations. It's not a humility which would make a human being feel sorry, or would cast down the degree of his prestige and honor—this would not make him despised or insulted. Can men be defined something other than seeker and appreciator of absolute beauty and perfection?

Therefore, it's only natural that men must put his forehead upon the dirt in front of such a source of absolute perfection, and must praise and adore that essence with his total existence. This praise and worship leads him towards the path of goodness, beauty, perfection, and he accordingly organizes his life's movement in that particular direction. Those, who have considered prayer and worship of Islam responsible for human disgrace and abjectness, and compared it to praising of sources of material powers, unfortunately did not appreciate and understand this delicate point that: The acts of praising and adoring goodness and purity in themselves are most powerful motivation for acquiring these virtues within the worshipper therefore the recital of—Glory to God—reminds us to aspire about these virtues in our own lives as well.

"All praises belong to God (Wal hamdu lillahi)!"

Throughout the tragic history of mankind, men because of miscellaneous consideration for obtaining small or big privileges—for living a few days longer, and in many cases just for the sake of living from hand to mouth—has allowed his tongue for praise and surrendered himself in humility in front of those who were exactly his equivalent, and by no means were possessors of superiority or distinction over him. Because men had imagined that bounties actually belonged to the bounty-users. In seeking these riches and possessions, he has accepted the bondage of their owners whether be it physical, spiritual or in mental form.

The reminder that all thanks and praises is reserved only for God and not for anybody else, makes us understand that all blessing riches, affluence, gifts, favor and bounties are from Him. Thus, in reality, no one other than God is owner of things which would authorize Him to enslave a fellow human being into bondage. It therefore, teaches to even those who are of rather weak determination, and whose hearts and eyes are seduced for riches and favors, not to attach any importance to insignificant favors and concessions awarded by holders of worldly power, position, and wealth. They should not consider these things awarded by them, rather the source of all blessings and bounties is God; and therefore, they should not allow themselves into servitude or bondage for the sake of those little favors or awards, tolerate deprivation for there genuine wants, and consider hoarders of these bounties as usurpers or aggressors.

"And there is no god but God (Wala ilahi illallahu)."

This is the slogan of Islam—a slogan which clearly and explicitly reflects in totality the world-view and ideological philosophy of Islamic school—it consists of one negation and one affirmation. Firstly, it negates all false deities, or powers other than God's. It frees everybody from the yoke of slavery of all devilish powers and cuts off each hand and shoulder, which try to pull him with different tricks towards the wrong path. It disassociates men from all sources and systems of power other than God's and from all motivations other than those liked by Him.

With this grand denial he free himself from all sorts of humilities, degradations, abject nesses, and bondages. Then he allows his inner-self to be ruled in accordance with God's will and command, which of course could be felt and executed under His administration in an ideal Islamic society. Such an acceptance and servitude in front of God is not comparable to any other type of servitude. Servitude of God means to arrange one's life logistic in accordance with His wisdom, and to live under His administration in an ideal Islamic society; whose real direction has been drawn in accordance with divine commands and also to endeavor with all power and means at one's disposal for materialization of such an ideal God's administration. Since other systems founded upon human intellectual thinking, are not free from factors such as human ignorance, lack of knowledge, crookedness, and most likely selfish motives can not help men succeed and lead himself towards the desired perfection.

Only God's administration and Islamic society, blessed with divine wisdom and providences is programmed according to human needs and requirements, as well as ways and means for fulfilling these requirements could provide suitable and favorable environment for the growth of that special creation called mankind. ***"We are not enemies of other systems, rather we are their sympathizers;"*** these are the words of God's messengers who are most concerned and sympathetic fatherly figures for mankind. They teach to all builders and designers of dwellings to be occupied by human beings, or in another word to all the leaders and founders of social systems that: ***"Men had never succeeded, nor will ever succeed or fulfill his desires in any other forms of ruling except Monotheistic System administered by God."*** History has proved, and we all have witnessed that in ungodly administrations how humanity has suffered and how horrible and wretched were the conditions of human beings under their oppressing regimes.

"And God is Great (Wallahu Akbar)."

After negating all false deities, an ordinary person still entangled by pagan tendencies feels lonely, stranger, and scared. On one side he witnesses sudden collapse of all mighty pagan infrastructures, which were stable till this very moment, and on the other hand paganism like a stable peak of mountain presents itself as a viable alternative, and tries its best to catch his attention. Those very things which he has negated, show their existence before his eyes and makes him scared. It's exactly at this point that he proclaims:

God is Great, greater than anybody or anything, greater than all the powers and their manifestations and He is beyond description. He is designer, creator of all natural and historical traditions, and divine laws of creation of this universe. Thus, ultimate victory lies with being compatible with these divine laws and traditions, and could only be achieved through being committed to divine commands. Only God's servants have been single victorious front throughout the historical struggle of mankind.

The Holy Prophet (SAW) comprehended and believed this historical reality correctly, and felt it with all power of his existence. It was because of this, reason that he single handedly stood up not only against all the deviated people of Mecca, but resisted the whole world. As it was genuinely expected from such an exalted personality, he resisted and remained steadfast to the extent that he was able to free the deviated caravan of humanity from bondage of worldly false powers, and directed it towards its natural path—the path of perfection and human-exaltation. Someone, who considers himself weak, timid, and indecisive against possessors of worldly powers, if he could realize that supreme power belongs to God; becomes calm, assured, and discovers the ignition of an exceptional kind of fire within his inner existence, transforming him into greatest and powerful person instantaneously. This was the summary of content of four sentences recited in standing position during the third and fourth units of prayer.

Chapter-14: Genuflection *(Rukoo)*[1]

Having recited the Holy Qur'an's [2] verses in the first and second unit or Four Praises *(Tasbihatul-Arba)* in third or fourth unit, in standing position, the worshipper enters into state of genuflection. He bows his head with respect to God, whose existence is the fountainhead of all supreme, exalted, and righteous virtues, which could be aspired by a human being. Genuflection reflects human-humility before a power, which he considers superior to himself. Because a Muslim considers God as the most supreme power, he performs genuflection in front of Him, and since he does not consider anyone other than God superior to him, he never bows his head in front of any body or anything. At the same time while he has lowered his head in humility in front of God, he also allows his tongue to recite His praise as follows:

"Glorified is my Lord, the cherisher of magnificent glory [3] (Sub hana rabbiyal'azime wa bihamdeh)."

This movement accompanied by recital of above sentence produces a feeling of servitude and bondage in front of God within a worshipper, as well as others who are witnessing this movement. Since God's servant could not belong to anybody else, therefore he openly and explicitly announces his honor, dignity, and freedom from the slavery of others.

1. Bowing in prayer before the state of Prostration

2. Recitation of verses in standing positions i.e. surahs the opening and the sincerity or another surah, in the first and second units; and recital of four praises or only surah praise in the third and fourth-units.

3. Instead of this praise, one may recite the following three times: ***"Glory be to God (Subhallallahi)."***

Chapter-15: Prostration *(Sujood)*

After raising his head from the state of genuflection, the worshipper is prepared to humiliate himself to the most extreme state in front of God through putting his forehead upon the dirt in the state of prostration. Placing one's forehead upon the ground (dirt)[1] is the highest degree of human humility, and worshipper considers this much humility appropriate in front of God. Because extreme servitude in front of God is tantamount to paying respect and bowing in front of absolute righteousness and absolute beauty. Such humiliation and servitude before anybody or anything other than Him is undesirable and strictly prohibited. Since with this action the jewel or essence of humanity—the most precious commodity in the bazaar of human existence—becomes shattered making a human being extremely lowered and undignified. While in the state of prostration, with his head upon dirt, his thoughts submerged in God's grandeur, his tongue also coordinates through reciting the following sentence of praise—announcing the interpretation of his action.

"Glorified is my Lord the cherisher of supreme glory (subhana rabbiyal a'la wa bihamdeh)." [2]

It's deserving for men only in front of an existence i.e. God, who is most supreme, decorated, and holy.... etc., to praise, worship, and lower himself until the state of prostration. Thus, prostration

---

1. In accordance with the Ahl al-Bayts (AS) School prostration is not allowed upon the wearable and eatable items and the Holy Prophet (SAW) always placed his forehead upon the dirt upon the ground. [Tr]

2. The worshipper may recite the praise Glory to God *(Subhanallah)* three times instead.

during prayer is not falling down upon dirt before an existence who is weak, finite, and incomplete, like bowing down in front of flimsy and hollow worldly powers; rather prostration means to put your forehead upon the dirt before a power which is supreme, holy, and magnificent. The worshipper with this act practically declares his obedience and surrender to a wise and seer God, and in reality before announcing to others he encourages and reminds his inner self to execute this submission and obedience in his own affairs. It's through this acceptance—absolute servitude in front of God—that men make himself free from slavery and bondage of everything and everybody and immunes himself from all sorts of imposed enslavements and insults. The most important influence expected from recitation of praises during genuflection and prostration stages is that it teaches worshipper that in front of which existence he must offer absolute surrender and adoration, simultaneously instructing him to negate, and prohibit these acts against anything or anybody except that single existence. There is a narration[1] quoted by Imam (AS) which describes relationship between the creator and created being in the state of prostration.

[1] The nearest state of communication between God and His servants is the state of Prostration.

—Safinatul Bihar, v-1, Chapter- Prostration.

Chapter-16: Witnessing *(Tashahud)*

In the second and last unit of each prayer, after raising head from second prostration, the worshipper in sitting position recites three sentences, each one of them reflects a basic reality of faith. This act of reciting these sentences is called the witnessing ***(tashahud)***. The first sentence consists of declaring I bear witness God's Unity:

"I bear witness that there is no god except God (Ashhadu anla ilaha illallah)."

"Only He (Wahdahu)" is the Lord of the Universe which in other words is described as follows:

"He has no partners or associates (La sharika lah)."

Whatever attraction whether be physical or material objects, or things which succeed in bringing men under their yoke of bondage, forcing him into servitude and obedience, could be rightly described as god for that person. Whims and passions, animal desires, greed and lusts, social contacts and systems, each one of them in special ways succeeds in trapping a human being into its bondage for providing services; and thus imposed its false godhood[1] upon that

---

[1] Refer to following of the Holy Qur'an's verses: ***"Hast thou seen him who maketh his desire his god, and God sendeth him astray purposely and sealeth up his hearing and his heart, and setteth on his sight a covering? Then who will lead him after God (hath condemned him). Will you not then heed?"***
—The Holy Qur'an (45:23).

"They have taken as lords besides God their rabbis and their monks and the Messiah son of Marry, when they were bidden to worship only one

trapped wretched fellow. There is no god but God negates all these types of servitudes and enslavements, and with the act of witnessing *(tashahud)*, the worshipper gives his testimony about this negation, i.e. he accepts that there is only one God, Who alone has the right of demanding absolute servitude and obedience, and everybody else other than Him, has absolutely no such rights upon men's neck.

If the above logic is accepted by someone, then naturally, he would never allow himself to surrender in front, and accept godhood of any other existences namely: human, animal, angelic, organic, inorganic, and whims and passions of self. Of course it does not mean that a Monotheist is against all social commitments and obligations or does not believe in any law or authority at all. Because it's obvious that social life is founded upon some inevitable obligations and obedience rather, it means that a Monotheist does not believe and tolerate any other order or administration, which is not based upon divine commands. In his individual or social life, he is attentive to divine orders; and often, in accordance with God's commands and relevant considerations for human life in social collective systems; it's obligatory upon him to obey someone in authority, and should also be responsible and committed to social responsibilities and obligations.

Thus, obedience and commitments being as characteristics of individual and social life are inseparable from the life of a Monotheist. But he does not surrender himself to whims and passions of his rebellious self or to selfish interests and egotism of individuals who are similar to him. Instead, his obedience is in front of a wise and seer God's commands. Because He is one Who prescribes laws and regulations which should be executed, and appoints holders of

---

God. There is no god save Him. Be He glorified from all that they ascribe as partner (unto Him)!"

—The Holy Qur'an (9:31).

"And Pharaoh said: O chiefs! I know not that ye have a god other than me, so kindle for me (afire), O Haman, to bake the mud; and set up for me a lofty tower in order that I may survey the god of Moses; and lo! I deem him of the liars."

—The Holy Qur'an (28:38).

authorities who in turns issue commands in accordance with divine instructions, for God's servants.[1] Following of the Holy Qur'an's verses explicitly explains the above fact:

"O ye who believe! Obey God, and Obey the messenger and those of you who are in authority; and if ye have a dispute concerning any matter, refer it to God and the messenger if ye are (in truth) believers in God and the Last Day. That is better and more seemly in the end."

—The Holy Qur'an (4: 59)

And probably it's for reflection of this reality that we recite the second sentence in the witnessing *(tashahud)* as follows:

"And I bear witness that Muhammad is His servant and prophet (Wa ashadu anna Muhammadan abduhu wa rasuluh)."

Acceptance of the Holy Prophet (SAW) as divine messenger is acceptance of God's representative or vicegerent or in other words, to search God's path through following his footsteps, and to receive divine commands through His appointed servant. There were plenty of God's worshippers who unfortunately made blunder in identifying the path desired by Him. Acceptance of the Holy Prophet (SAW) as His prophet explicitly defines direction for actions and endeavourers. Such movement is desirable in a believer's life to prove his true commitments for God's worshipping. In the above sentence through using word servant or a slave before the word prophet, special emphasis has been attached to the Holy Prophet's (SAW) servant hood. It seems as if the aim was to introduce most

---

1. In this regard please refer to the following verses of the Holy Qur'an:

"Whoso obeyeth the messenger; obeyeth God, and whoso turneth away: We have not sent thee as a warder over them."

—The Holy Qur'an (4: 80).

"Your friends can be only God; and His messenger and those who believe, who establish worship and pay the poor due and bow down (in prayer)."

—The Holy Qur'an (5: 55).

supreme and important characteristic of Islam, which indeed is—***all human virtues may be summarized in being the real sincere slave of God. In accordance with the Islamic beliefs one who is ahead of others in this field is heaviest on balance or scale of humanity.***

One who is aware of meanings of being God's slave, does not require logical or rational explanation to support the above reality. If bondage to God means to surrender in front of infinite wisdom, insight, blessing, righteousness, and beauty, and is accompanied with freedom from self's slavery and from everything and everybody other than God, could there be any virtue superior to this? Is it not true that all evilness, degradation, wretchedness, meanness, cowardice, and darkness result from bondage of men to rebellion of his self *(nafs)*. Is it not true that bondage to God, destroys and burns roots of all other sorts of servitude.

The above-mentioned two sentences recited in the witnessing *(tashahud)* contain a very delicate and exact point, which is: The worshipper takes a testimony about God's Unity and about prophet hood, i.e. he witnesses that there is no god but God, and further confirms servant hood and prophet hood of the Holy Prophet (SAW). This testimony in reality, means acceptance of all commitments and obligations related to the above two beliefs. As if the worshipper with this testimony wants to say—that I am willing to assume all responsibilities upon my shoulders resulting from the above two beliefs; God's Unity *(towheed)*, and prophet hood *(nabuwwat)*. A characterless and hollow knowledge without commitment, belief, and action does not possess any value from Islamic point of view. To witness a reality means, to stand for it and acceptance of all commitments, responsibilities, and obligations resulting therein, an acceptance arising out of a pure, sincere, and positive belief. Thus, recital of the witnessing *(tashahud)* in prayer is like taking an oath of allegiance through the worshipper before God and His prophet. The third sentence of witnessing *(tashahud)* is a request and a supplication as follows:

"O God, bless Muhammad and his progeny (Allahumma salli'ala Muhammadin wa aale Muhammad)."

The Holy Prophet (SAW) and his holy progeny are perfect and complete manifestations of this school of thought. Worshipper through reciting this supplication makes refreshing his memory about those perfect ideals, and praising them strengthens his spiritual union with them. Followers of each school or ideology, if do not see real models or perfect manifestations of that particular school of thought, are likely to follow wrong courses and may get lost. It's therefore through such live presentation of real manifestations, that has insured permanency of school of divine prophets throughout the course of time. History bears witness that there were many ideologues or thinkers, who for assuring superior and prosperous life for mankind, presented various schemes and designs of Utopian Perfect City *(Medina-Fazileh)*, and wrote voluminous books writings in support of their proposals. But the divine prophets, instead of indulging themselves into philosophical debates, presented their designs by their actions.

Through presenting themselves as perfect models, as well as showing noble deeds of their prime disciples, the divine prophets succeeded to produce ideal perfect human beings *(insan-e-kamil)*, upon whose shoulders rested the structure of divine schools; and this was the reason that the schools of divine prophets remained immortal forever, while nothing except some writings and impressions on the pages of books were left from the plans and designs of those great philosophers and thinkers. The worshipper for the Holy Prophet (SAW) and his holy progeny, who were most ideal manifestations of this school, sincerely offers supplications. He sends greetings to ones, who spent their entire lives as ideals of this school, and presented balanced perfect human beings of Islam to the history. Worshipper sends salutations and blessing for them and requests the same from God. In this way he tries to strengthen his spiritual union with them; the union which provides a powerful force and motivates him to follow the path and ideals so cherished by them.

Sending blessings and salutations for the Holy Prophet (SAW) and his Holy Progeny (AS) means to pay homage to most ideal, perfect, and selected personalities of Islam. With manifestations of these ideals and perfect individuals in the eyes of his mind, a Muslim could always identify the path he should follow, and make himself ready for moving in that direction.

Chapter-17: Salutations *(Salam)*

Salutation in prayer consists of sending three greetings[1] and of course it's accompanied with the Name and God's remembrance. Thus, prayer starts in the Name of God and ends with His Name, and between the beginning and end, there is nothing except His remembrance and Name. If there is a sentence praising the Holy Prophet (SAW) and his Holy Progeny (AS), even this is accompanied with God, and seeking His help through His blessings and favors. The first sentence is a salutation by worshipper to the Holy Prophet (SAW), God, seeking His blessings and favors upon him:

"Peace be upon you, O Apostle, and mercy and blessings of God be upon him. (Assalamu alayka ayyuhan' nabiyyu wa rahmatullahi wa barakatuh)."

The Holy Prophet (SAW) is the founder of Islam, he is responsible for all actions, efforts, and endeavourers for the sake of this movement, which are also cherished by worshipper. He was proclaimer of Monotheism and shook conscience of world, and laid down foundation of a decent life for mankind forever. He was designer of perfect Islamic human being, and Islamic society which will continue to produce such ideal personalities. Now worshipper with his prayer and relevant lessons and guidance therein, reflects same slogan in his own life for his own environment and period. He takes a giant step towards that superior and perfect society prescribed by that exalted personality–the Holy Prophet (SAW). Therefore, it is natural that, when worshipper is about to finish this act, he remembers the Holy Prophet (SAW) with a salutation and regards, who has guided him towards this path and has been

1. Out of these three only the last one is mandatory and the other two are optional.

his leader throughout the journey; and in this manner he announces his presence along with him, and on his path. In the second sentence of salutations, worshipper sends his regards and greetings upon him, his fellow combatants, and upon all righteous servants of God:

"Peace be upon us and all righteous servants of Good (As salamu alayna wa ala ibadillahis salihin)."

Therefore, in this way he keeps the memory of God's righteous servants alive in his mind and feeling of their presence and existence provides him strength and energy. In a world where manifestations of sin: Abjectness, ugliness, savageries, tyranny, defilement, and uncleanness have overtaken every place and everybody; where, looking from the eyes of an intelligent, aware, and conscious person, present environment presents a picture of total bankruptcy of all human values. Where emptiness, hollowness, and fatigue is covered through artificial glittering. In a world, where just and truth seeking voices are silenced through disgracing deeds of selfish and ambitious persons, where positions hold by noble personalities such as Imam Ali (AS), Imam al-Husain (AS.), and Imam al-Sadiq (AS) are filled with demagogic uproar of persons like Muawiyeh, Yazid, and Mansoor; and in summary, in a world where Satan's unworthy sons have occupied all places once held by God's righteous servants. In such state of affairs is there any hope or expectation that righteousness and goodness would have any chance to prevail?

Can any other thing except sin, defilement, disappointment, and injustice be expected from human beings? One must accept that if there is a possibility to change things it can not be done easily. Greetings and salutations to God's worthy and righteous servants of, who under such dark environment provide comforts and take care of all hopeless and heartbroken people. As if it's like a glad tidings for bright light arising out of the heart of total darkness. It promises the worshipper about existence and presence of other fellow combatants. It tells him: You are not alone in this dry desert, you may find fruitful and long lasting sprouts. As always is the case in history, that extremely deviated and corrupt societies, were also the birth places of most determined, will-powered and famous reformers who laid down foundation for a new refreshing life-giving ideologies, and established new systems in the midst of all that hopelessness and darkness.

Even now, in accordance with historical divine traditions, same enlightened forces of righteousness and goodness, in the midst of this world full of darkness and corruption are involved actively. Yes! The righteous servants of God, who consider God worthy and deserving for worship, follow His command and confront and resist false claimers of godhood *(taqhoot).* Who are these decent servants of God and where can they be found? Should not a lesson be learned from them and should not they he accompanied in their forward march? Yes. When worshipper placed himself along with these worthy individuals and sends greetings for himself as well as for themselves a ray of pride, honor, and assurance shines in his heart.

He tries his best truly to join their rank to place himself along with them, and since he could not march step by step along with them, feels sorry about it, this feeling bestows upon him a fresh commitment and obligation. What types of individuals are these worthy righteous servants and what is worthiness supposed to be? Worthiness does not mean simply offering prayers only. A worthy human being is one, who is able to discharge heavy divine responsibilities in a proper manner, as befitting and as expected from a God's sincere servant. In other words he may be compared to an ideal worthy student in a class, who is supposed to do his homework well. In the end in third sentence, worshiper sends greeting to same worthy servants to angles or other worshippers as follows:

"Peace be upon you, and the mercy and blessing of God! (Assalamu alaykum wa rahmatullahi wa barakatuh)·"

Therefore, in this manner worshipper reminds himself about goodness and worthiness or angelic virtues or union with other worshippers, and thus, finishes his prayer through offering supplications and greetings for his respected audience.

GLOSSARY

1. (SAW): S'ALLALLAAHU A'LAYHI WA AALIHEE WA SALLAM

   (O God send salutations upon Muhammad and his family)

2. (AS): A'LAYHIS SALAM

   (Salutations be upon him)

3. (SA): SALAWAATULLAAHI A'LAYHAA

   (Salutations be upon her)

4. (RA): Rizwan Allah Aleh.

   (May God be pleased with him).

5. (AF): Ajjallaho Farjeh

   (May God Hasten His Appearance).

Ahl al-Bayt (AS) Islamic Cultural Services (AICS) of N.A.

"ANA MADINATAUL-ILMI WA ALIYUAN BABUHA"

"I am the City of Knowledge & Ali is the Gate"

—The Holy Prophet (PBUH)

"In the Name of Allah, the most Beneficent and the most Merciful"

OUR MISSION STATEMENT

1. "Wealth and children are an ornament of this life of the world; but the good deeds (Baqyat-as-Salehat) which endure are better in thy Lord's sight for reward and better in respect of hope; O ye who believe! If you help Allah's cause, He will help you and will make your foothold firm; 3-"As for those who strive in Us, We surely guide them to our path, and lo! Allah is with the good."

—The Holy Qur'an (18:46, 47:07, 29:69).

4. It has been narrated that the (Eight) Imam al-Rida (A.S) has said to one of his followers. ***"May Allah bless the servant who keeps our vicegerency (vilayat) alive."*** The follower asked him: ***'How they could be kept alive?'*** ***"The truth and goodness of our sayings, realities of our traditions and profundities of our knowledge should be properly introduced and explained to the people that means keeping the affairs of our vicegerency (vilayat) alive."*** **Replied the imam (A.S)**

—Bihar al-Anwar, v. 2, page-30, Narration # 13.

5. Martyr Allameh Murtaza Mutaheri (R.A) has said: ***"We are responsible people; we have not produced sufficient literature in various aspects of Islam in current languages. Had we therefore made available the pure and sweet waters in abundance, people would not have contented themselves with polluted waters."***

6. In the aftermath of recent uprisings in the Middle East and Noth Africa, there is a genuine curiosity among the International Community to be enlightened about Islam in general and especially about the School of—Ahl al- Bayt (A.S).

7. The Holy Prophet (SAW) has narrated that: "I am leaving two heavy trusts among you i.e. the book of God and my Ahl al-Bayt, who would never separate from each other until they would meet me at the Stream of Kauther in the Paradise; hold tight to both of them tightly in order to achieve salvation."

8. Therefore the purpose of this organization is translation and publication of books regarding the Knowledge and Learning of Ahl al-Bayt (AS) in English so that the intellectuals and researches, university scholars, and all the seekers of truth should have access to these published books.

O Allah! Please send Salutations to the Holy Prophet Muhammad and His Holy Progeny.

Phone: (407) 470-3518

Fax: (407) 352-3694

E-mail:

alamdar_zaidi2000@yahoo.com

Address:

8013 Bright Court , Orlando, FL32836 (USA)

Sayyid Hussein Alamdar P.E, holds a MSCE from the University of South Carolina, at Columbia, S.C. He served Duke Power Company, Charlotte N.C from 1971-1982. In 1983, he was invited to join the Water and Power Co in Tehran, where he served as a Project Manager for Hydroelectric Projects until 2003. During his stay in Iran for 20 year (1983-2003) in addition to his engineering responsibilities he was blessed with the Divine grace of also attending Islamic Seminary under the able tutorship of Ayatollah Seyed Mohammad Taqi Hakim Shooshtari and Hajj Aghai Ali Solemani Aashtiani in Tehran. He also founded the Ahl al-Bayt Islamic Cultural Services (AICS) of USA to accomplish the following exalted objectives to publish the *Uloom & Mu'arif* of Ahl al-Bayt (AS): *1. It has been narrated that Imam al-Rida (A.S) has said to one of his followers: "May Allah bless the servant who keeps our vicegerency (vilayat) alive through publication of our learning (mu'arif) and knowledge (uloom)."*

Alamdar, has translated the following books, some of them are also available on the internet at WWW. Al-Islam.org, Islamic Library Project of Stanford University California (USA). His translated books are also being published by the Author house of Bloomington, Indiana, USA and are being marketed through Amazon.com and Burns and Nobles as a hard copy, soft copy, and kindle book.

1. **Self Building (Khud Sazi wa Tahzib wa Tazkiyeh Nafs): Ayatollah Ibrahim Amini**

2. **Truth and Falsehood: Martyr Ayatollah Murtaza Motaheri (RA)**

3. **Importnce of Patience and Prayer: Grand Ayatollah Seyed Ali Khamenei**

4. Spiritual Journeys of the Mystics (Saluk-e-Arifan): Grand Ayatollah Malaki Tabrizi (RA)

5. Etiquette of the Holy Month of Ramadan: Grand Ayatollah Malaki Tabrizi (RA)

6. Radiance of Vicegerency (Frooghe-e-Vilayat): Grand Ayatollah J'afar Sobhanie

7. Shi'i Replies to Wahabi Questions: Grand Ayatollah J'afar Sobhanie

8. The Story of Karbala: Ayatollah Ali Nazari Munfarid

9. How to Bridge the Generation Gap: Ayatollah Seyed Muhammad Taqi Hakim

10. Imam al-Zain al-A'abedin (AS): Seyed Munthir Hakim

11. Imam al-Baqir (AS): Seyed Munthir Hakim

12. Biography of Ash Sharif ar-Radi: Muhammad Ibrahim Nejad

13. History of the Holy Mosque of Jamkaran

14. Translation of the Death-Will (Vasiyat Nameh) of Grand Ayatollah Seyed Muhammad Rida Golpaygani

15. Every Must Know (Hame Bayad Bedanand): Ayatollah Ibrahim Amini

16. Fatimeh al-Zahra (SA): Seyed Munthir Hakim

17. Imam Jafar al-Sadiq (AS): Seyed Munthir Hakim

Please visit the following websites:
http://www.amazon.com/author/sayyidalamdar
http://www.sayyidalamdar.com

A Request from the Translator

Dear Readers: Please recite Surah al-Fatihah for the exalted souls of the Holy Prophet (SAW), his Ahl al-Bayt (AS), all divine messengers, all the diseased believing men and women (momeneens wa momenaat), and especially for (Late) Mir Liyaqat Ali Zaidi, (Late) Seyedeh Ashrafun Nisa Begum, and Ali Zaidi a proactive and pious youth of Shi'i community of Seattle, WA who lost his precious life in a car accident last year.

Thanks!

Index

***

Printed in the United States
By Bookmasters